Learning Rebooted

Arguing that education systems are failing to keep up with the pace of change in society, *Learning Rebooted: Education Fit for the Digital Age* sets out a unique proposal for system-wide radical change. Focusing on the transformations needed in order to align education systems with current trends in society, the book stimulates discussion by offering a heightened understanding of what education reform needs to look like, and suggesting a way forward for both individual schools and whole systems.

The book makes a clear delineation between learning and education, building a case for how learning, an essential skill, is often not allowed to flourish in many modern education systems. Chapters explore how rapid changes to technology are shaping the way young people share, collaborate and communicate and, arguing that education systems continue to produce young people who are not equipped with the skills that society needs, the book makes a cogent case for how education systems need to reflect these profound changes, as well as highlighting how Learning Organisations could rationalise their expenditure on technology.

This unique and radical book brings topical issues to the forefront of discussion, and is essential reading for school leaders, policymakers and governors.

James Penny is Founder and Director of The Original Group, UK, which works with a range of organisations and individuals seeking to break new ground in education, business and technology.

Learning Rebooted

Education Fit for the Digital Age

James Penny

Routledge
Taylor & Francis Group

LONDON AND NEW YORK

First published 2018
by Routledge
2 Park Square, Milton Park, Abingdon, Oxon OX14 4RN

and by Routledge
711 Third Avenue, New York, NY 10017

Routledge is an imprint of the Taylor & Francis Group, an informa business

British Library Cataloguing in Publication Data
A catalogue record for this book is available from the British Library

Library of Congress Cataloging in Publication Data
A catalog record for this book has been requested.

ISBN: 978-0-8153-6828-1 (hbk)
ISBN: 978-0-8153-6830-4 (pbk)
ISBN: 978-1-351-25524-0 (ebk)

Typeset in Melior
by Sunrise Setting Ltd., Brixham, UK

MIX
Paper from
responsible sources
FSC
www.fsc.org FSC™ C013985

Printed in the United Kingdom
by Henry Ling Limited

Dedication – to the people who matter

This book would not have been possible without my wife who had the faith to support and encourage me to take on this challenge, and gave me the time and space to develop the ideas whilst providing thoughts and ideas as the manuscript developed. Inspiration also came from my children who, through their curiosity and zest for life, renew the vigour and passion I have for learning every day and inspire in me the feeling that anything is possible.

The vast majority of this book was written whilst we lived in the peace and tranquillity of the Dorset countryside. It would be hard to get further from the hustle and bustle of modern life than 'Life on the Hill' as we call it. The location provided space to think, time to reflect and inspiration from the ancient landscape. The proximity of Bronze Age bowl-barrow burial sites have spoken to the continuous habitation of the area for over 4000 years. As I write about learning, this direct proximity to our ancestors provides a tangible link to how we have developed through our desire to learn.

Contents

Foreword

Our education systems are broken and we are not doing enough to mend them. Too often learning is being suppressed under an industrial education system that can squash creativity, mitigate against developing the skills that our learners need to be successful and can often fail to recognise the social challenges faced everyday by some in society. There are pockets of excellence where educators and leaders are creating structures and organisations that are addressing the real needs of learners, but these pockets are too few and they are not expanding fast enough. The educators and business leaders who are creating real change are not being supported to bring about the revolution that is required. We must do more and we must do it quickly. Reform that takes years wastes the potential of whole cohorts of learners who could contribute so much to our society.

Politicians and leaders appear to be in denial about some of the profound changes taking place in society, especially the massive change that technology is bringing about in every part of our lives. This is not just about teaching skills in coding or technology-related qualifications. The challenge goes much deeper. If in one breath we are teaching coding but with the next breath we are banning personal devices from the learning environment then what messages do we send to our learners? If in Learning Organisations we continue to build 20th-century local area networks instead of secure connected global systems, then no amount of understanding of coding will make a difference. I applaud what the University Technical College movement is doing in England – it is focusing learning around the technology revolution – but we must go further. We need system-wide reform on the same scale, as with the reforms that created the National Health Service (NHS) and universal education for all in the middle of the 20th century.

In the UK, our mathematicians laid the foundations for the creation of the computer, and our research scientists defined the protocols that power the World Wide Web. A small company with its roots in a school-based computer revolution in the mid-1980s now produces the designs for microprocessors that power the vast majority of mobile devices on the planet. The company? ARM Holdings, with its roots in the BBC microcomputer. Our creative people lead the way in many areas. The design guru Jonathan Ive is responsible for Apple designs that have helped make the company the largest in the world by market capitalisation in 2016. We can get education right for everyone. But it's going to take a mighty effort and a lot of people working together.

This is a book about how learning sits within our society. It is about how our education systems need to simultaneously reflect and lead society, providing what society needs our learners to know and understand. In the following chapters I aim to tease out how learning has been contextualised within the social fabric of our society. To frame the discussion, I reflect on three ages in history and how learning has developed in response to the changes taking place in society. These ages are the *pre-industrial age*, the *industrial age* and the *post-industrial age*. Much of the text reflects on the significant changes taking place in our current era – a time marked by the rapid changes to the way we communicate and share, an age that will be remembered for the rapid rise of digital devices and an age in which the pace of change is creating significant fractures in society.

On a personal level, after spending thirty-two years working in and around education, a number of themes kept emerging in a wide range of contexts. Not all were immediately connected and not all related to the job I was doing at the time. However, they all had a thread of learning running through them and they started to coalesce into something that resonated strongly with discussions about education reform. So, in late 2015 I decided it was time to leave my job – not an easy decision after thirty-two years of employment – and explore these themes. I needed time to explore the ideas, to create the links between what initially appeared to be unrelated ideas and to craft the text of this book to share with a wider audience some of the exceptional learning I have seen over the years. But more than just sharing what is good, *I want to call loudly for the system-wide reform that our learners deserve.* As I write this book we find ourselves in the middle of an extraordinary set of events concerning our education system in England. Our young people are being forced into taking summative tests that many parents and educators see as having little or no value. Twice already, we have seen test papers and answers being posted online before students even take the test. As I will explore in the following chapters, this is not surprising. Knowledge is no longer in the hands of the few. Technology has democratised knowledge ownership and we all have the *right to roam* over global data repositories. Some fundamental social truths that have held for generations are being eroded or have changed beyond recognition, but our education systems are struggling to keep up.

As I travelled and discussed education in a wide variety of contexts over the last ten years, there was a view that long-established education systems were not providing for the needs and aspirations of learners. Reform was needed but was going to be very challenging – so deeply ingrained were some of the ideas that needed to change. But as I travelled and talked to policymakers, students, teachers, education leaders, business leaders and wise colleagues, it was evident that there were areas where the system was clearly *not* broken. These included places where new organisational structures were being put in place that were focused around the needs of the learners. One of the most notable areas was London, where the London Challenge, launched in 2003, focused specifically on transforming schools in the capital. The policy inspired new structures to emerge with a focus on the needs of the local community. That policy has had a marked effect on achievement for learners in London in terms of examination outcomes. This example shows how significant differences can be made to the lives and *life chances* of learners. But even when we take London as an example, the changes being made struggle to scale effectively across even the UK. Excellent as the London Challenge was, I could travel twenty miles down the road and see poor-quality education and learning that was not inspiring and not providing what our young people needed. How could these small areas of excellence scale? What was it that had come together to convince these educators that things needed to be done differently? When I talk about 'significant difference' I am referencing improved outcomes in agreed benchmarks like end-of-stage examinations, increased levels of literacy and numeracy, and judgements from inspections. But there is more. These pockets of excellence were also exploring the significance of working outside the accepted norms of school days that run from 8:30 am to 3:30 pm. One organisation that sprung up to run a group of schools took as their mission the need to bring together education with social care. The aim was to make sure that students and families had access to the full range of social services in an easily accessible way to help meet their needs. Some of the changes encountered used tools and method-ologies that some would consider revolutionary rather than evolution-ary. They were looking at approaches that had not been sanctioned by policy; indeed, some clandestinely operated contrary to the officially sanctioned approaches whilst still showing improvement in outcomes. They were using ideas that were transposed from a wide variety of areas that, traditionally, education did not explore. I've shared these themes of change and working differently throughout the book, with some specific examples of where education organisations are making a real difference to the lives of learners every day. But they are doing so by working outside the accepted norms and by challenging themselves to be different for the sake of learning.

Across the developed world, the aspiration for equality of access to education has been embraced and funded largely from public finances. In developing economies, the aspiration is to provide access to edu-cation for all young people, with further and higher education seen as a roadway to success. No one denies that access to learning is not a worthy aspiration, but so often the education systems fall short of the dreams we hold for our learners.

Why are there pockets of excellence? Why don't those examples of excellence grow outwards and light up all the corners of an education system? Why do we still see Learning Organisations that are failing their communities? As I'll explore in this book, I believe that education sys-tems are struggling to keep up with the speed of change. Those that can keep up are doing an excellent job. But keeping up relies on highly effective leadership and those leaders are in short supply. The current approach to policymaking is too slow and cumbersome. It is reactive and not proactive. Therefore, the challenge that is required at the system level is often lacking. Those who can grasp hold of the opportunities that current policy offers can make a difference, but they need to be entre-preneurs, risk-takers and supremely self-confident. Those that wait for the system to guide them do not get the support they need. Also, the underlying social truths that have driven education for decades are eroding faster than we care to admit. Our modern data-driven world is capable of sharing ideas almost instantly. With that sharing comes the possibility for entrepreneurs to spot opportunities and bring goods and services to the marketplace in weeks rather than months or years. Generally, government is wary of new technology. Maybe the tools are still not mature enough, although that appears not to be the case. Whilst journalists are now routinely seen with a tablet device as they speak to the camera (so they can get the latest information instantly), the majority of politicians and those who support them still rely on paper notes and written documentation. Whilst progress is being made, it is too slow. In the UK, some brave attempts to transform public services with technology have failed. But these failures are mostly down to the way systems were commissioned rather than to the technology itself. If a global banking system that transfers billions of currency units around the world each day can reliably function in the digital world, then it is not beyond a nation state to do so. Most of the time, tradition is an asset; in the digital age, it can be the opposite.

In the chapters that follow I want to share some of the things that drive learning and that have shaped education systems. I'll argue that some of the fundamental building blocks that underpin our education systems in the past have become irrelevant and have not been replaced by the new social truths. I will argue that processes and organisational structures that were highly relevant in the past need reinterpreting for the current age and that there are places, people and organisations that have successfully managed this reinterpretation and are delivering high-quality and relevant learning. None of the stagnation in policy, process and organisational structures has been intentional. On the contrary, much of the confusion comes about as an unintended consequence of policy or from well-meaning interventions that work only in specific contexts but have been championed as the way ahead for all, only to fall a long way short of the outcomes that are hoped for. I'll also look at how our educators are leading the revolution in schools, colleges and universities. Despite what we might hear in the popular media, educators are at the forefront of change, working with and responding to the needs of their learners. Sometimes they come up against what appear to be insurmountable barriers, but in the true spirit of learning they find a way round, through or over the barriers.

1 What is this book?

This book is a reflection of what we see around us. The text seeks to examine in more depth some of the things that are commonly accepted about learning. By looking more deeply at what is really happening and by accepting some of the changes that are clearly visible, a new vision for learning starts to emerge – one that can appear to be at odds with what is commonly accepted to be true. Take the way that young people are flocking to YouTube as the place of choice to find things out. Remove the myth that everything they do there is bad or subversive and take time to look at some of the positive things that emerge. Take time to watch and reflect on some of the video blogs that are being posted and, as with all things, take time to sort the good from the bad. Just because something is self-published does not make it automatically bad or of poor quality. For years we have operated with newspapers and other publications that seek to put across a particular viewpoint. We have become accustomed to reading these publications with an under-standing of their political or personal viewpoints. Watching, reading and listening to digital media is no different. The real change is the quantity and speed of dissemination.

This is not a history book. I've tried as carefully as I can to place key historical facts against the framework of the discussion. But the detailed analysis of historical events is not what I have set out to achieve. The vast majority of 'History of Education' books broadly concentrate on the development of education organisations like schools, colleges and universities against the backdrop of history with a keen focus on how the political process affects the education that young people receive. Many of these books offer an excellent overview of how formal learning developed, but tend to give less of an overview of the broader social context. This is not a book about technology per se, but it does explore some of the fundamental technological developments that have shaped the changes we see in society. It is impossible to explore contemporary society and learning without a discussion on technology. Technology has fundamentally changed how our world works. It has had profound effects on every aspect of life. Education systems are one of the last areas of society to reflect and respond to these changes. To better understand the changes we are seeing, I will explore trends and ideas that are shaping society, the impact of technology on the changes we are seeing and how these changes relate to learning.

Throughout the following text I have used certain words in very specific ways. To help in reading what follows, I have provided a set of definitions. I do not want to get tied up in semantics but neither do I want to assume everyone has the same definitions as I do.

Definitions

Learning – What everyone does all the time. We experiment, build tools and explore. Learning is innate and does not need to be taught. Learning does not just happen in 'Learning Organisations' (see definition below), but all the time, and never stops from birth to death.

Learners – Anyone who has the need to learn – and that's all of us! I do not discriminate by age and I view learners as being of any age. At times in the book I will look at younger learners, and when I do I will ensure that I make it clear that this is the subset I am talking about.

Learning Organisations – We hear talk of schools, colleges and university. There are multiple types of schools, from academies to free schools to university technical colleges to independent schools, and the list goes on. There is post-16 provision and higher education. So, I intend the phrase 'Learning Organisation' to mean anywhere learners come together to learn or where learning takes place.

Education – Whilst the word has it roots in Latin, with a very specific meaning, within the current education environment the word 'education' is frequently used to describe what goes on in Learning Organisations. We talk of an education system as a descriptor for the structures and organisations that a region or country dictates for its learners. Education is more often used in this context than it is in the context of its original roots.

Curriculum – What an education systems dictates should be taught to learners. A curriculum is typically delineated by age and is logically constructed to build depth of understanding in a specific topic, area or discipline. There are, in fact, multiple definitions of what a curriculum is and reviewing the assumptions that drive a specific definition gives a fascinating insight into the fundamental beliefs that people hold about what an education system should deliver.

IT – Information Technology. Anything that uses a microprocessor to process data. A while back someone put a 'C' between the I and T and we got ICT with the 'C' standing for Communications, giving us Information Communications Technology.

Smartphone – There was a time when a phone transmitted voice calls using technology that translated analogue sound waves into electrical signals. But with the advent of the microprocessor, the analogue sound waves got translated into digital data sets. All other IT worked by transferring digital data sets and, therefore, voice calls simply became another digital data set. Once this had happened, voice and other data could use the same transmission medium – namely, the Internet (see below) – and what started as a phone became a personal computer that could do many things. Thus, the smartphone was born. Roughly, this occurred in the late 1980s and early 1990s, but it really took off when Apple launched the first iPhone in 2007. This introduced the first really usable touch interface and combined the functionality of a phone with a computer to support easy browsing of the Web as well as listening to music, along with other innovations.

Internet – A global network of connected computer systems. The Internet has existed since the early 1970s when universities and the military recognised that the ability to share data across the world instantly provided significant advantage. Not to be confused with . . .

The World Wide Web – A set of protocols defined by Tim Berners-Lee and a team at CERN in the early 1990s that defined a language allowing users to simply and easily publish text, images and other media in a way that other users could read, copy and interact with. The Web relies on the Internet to operate, and as wireless connectivity develops, the networks established by mobile operators are providing an essential element to empowering the revolution of the Web.

The evolution of technology

Technology evolves constantly – we all know that. But there are times when tipping points occur. These are points where certain technologies mature, price points drop due to efficiencies in production of predicted volumes and, therefore, what was previously impossible becomes either technically possible, financially viable or both.

In the context of learning, the real revolution started in 2006 when processor architectures matured to support microprocessors that used much less power. This allowed devices to do more things whilst consuming less power and a revolution was started. Several global companies took advantage of this confluence of technology and price point, and reliable tablets were produced that had a simple user interface (UI) that allowed users to interact through touch. Arguably, Apple was the first organisation to take significant advantage of these developments. Because they controlled both the hardware and the software, they were able to maximise the technical developments whilst the price point was not such an issue with their established user base. This revolution in UI design changed the face of mobile computing. The mature touch interface that Apple launched with iOS and the similar UI that Google launched with Android has changed the face of computing. Suddenly the traditional keyboard disappeared in favour of an on-screen version that appeared and disappeared as needed, opening up a much larger area of screen space than was possible with a design that had to include a traditional physical keyboard. Since 2010, when the first commercially viable portable tablet devices came to market, the complexity of technology and the breadth of choice has rapidly developed.

Enabling Technologies

As I look across the technology world I see what I have called a set of 'Enabling Technologies'. These are technologies that are being used by backroom start-ups and global corporations alike. These technologies are enabling new innovations and supporting entrepreneurs to develop new and exciting business models. These Enabling Technologies are well established and are supported by a well-defined roadmap; they underpin our society and are defining new social truths about how society operates and how services are being delivered to every person, irrespective of age, gender, race or orientation. These technologies are equivalent to the infrastructure that we laid down in the pre-industrial and industrial ages. In the pre-industrial age, tracks and roads enabled communication, and in the industrial era, the canals, railways and roads were essential infrastructure. Telephones and wired communications heralded the start of the communications revolution that is now pervasive.

Mobile connectivity

Without connectivity, no matter how smart your mobile device is, you are at a disadvantage. At the same time as the touch UI was being rolled out there were significant developments taking place in wireless networks, both at the level of adding wireless provision to existing physical locations and in the development of mobile networks. With third generation (3G) and then fourth generation (4G) networks, the potential to access complex data sets and documents whilst moving between locations became not only possible but also very simple. Devices are now capable of automatically connecting. With this development came the almost ubiquitous roll-out of free Wi-Fi in locations as diverse as coffee shops, shopping complexes, public buildings and private business buildings.

Cloud

The exact derivation of the term 'cloud' is not clear, but it emerged around 2010. At one level, it's an interesting metaphor for where your documents are stored when you are never in one physical location and, as such, the term has taken on a mythical status as a way of describing where and how data is stored. However, at the more technical level the National Institute for Standards in Technology (NIST), a US-based standards organisation, published a short paper in November 2011 that clarified the key attributes of cloud computing. This defined Infrastructure, Software and Platform as a Service (IaaS, SaaS, PaaS) and the three models for cloud deployment: public, private and hybrid. These definitions have subsequently been adopted as the intellectual underpinning for cloud computing. Beware of those who talk about the cloud but have never heard of the NIST definitions – they might just be talking hype without any real understanding of the fundamental nature of the shift that cloud computing has created and will continue to create.

Mobility

As processors became more powerful yet less power hungry, it became possible to build devices that have multiple functions in a form factor that was small enough and light enough to be personal and mobile. This set in motion the 'second mobile revolution' as I call it. The first revolution was with laptop devices. These were, however, always expensive and relatively heavy and cumbersome. We were never going to get to a point where everyone had a laptop computer. Whereas with smartphones and other such devices the possibility of personal ownership is not only possible because of the price point but practical in terms of portability. Like the traditional wristwatch, everyone can have a Smart device.

IPv6

With the explosion of mobility and the increasing development of connectivity comes another problem: millions of organisations, groups and people wanted to create websites. The Web has become the essential 'marketing' tool for millions of companies and billions of people. From online shopping, to information about goods and services, to accessing public services, to accessing learning, the Web is the de facto place to go. However, every time we create a website, a web presence or want to uniquely address a device attached to the Internet we need a unique way of identifying that presence. This is achieved by using what is called an internet protocol (IP) address. A series of numbers that, put simply, translate into a way for the Internet to route your request for data to the right location. The challenge was that the original pool of IP addresses was running out; there were only about 4 billion addresses, which is a lot but nowhere near enough. In effect, there was a finite limit to the number of websites that could be uniquely identified and to the number of devices that could be uniquely identified. So IPv6 was implemented. This protocol provides for . . . , well, the number is big, so big that it uses numbers that most people don't even know exist. In mathematical terms, the number is 3.4×10^{38}. In longhand that's 340,282,366,920,938,463,463,374,607,431,768,211,456, which, if you want to say it, is apparently: three hundred and forty undecillion, two hundred and eighty-two decillion, three hundred and sixty-six nonillion, nine hundred and twenty octillion, nine hundred and thirty-eight septillion, four hundred and sixty-three sextillion, four hundred and sixty-three quintillion, three hundred and seventy-four quadrillion, six hundred and seven trillion, four hundred and thirty-one billion, seven hundred and sixty-eight million, two hundred and eleven thousand, four hundred and fifty-six! Suffice it to say we are safe for a few years yet.

The World Wide Web

Alongside the wheel, electricity and antibiotics, the Web is one of the greatest inventions of all time. It is a true Enabling Technology for me because although the protocols that defined the Web were created in the early 1990s (see the Definitions section above) it was not until connectivity, mobility and cloud technologies emerged that the Web was able to be exploited to the extent it is today. In effect, it sat there for nearly ten years being slowly used more and more before the explosion in mobility in the early 2000s and the continued explosion of the 'second mobility revolution' from 2010 onwards saw a massive growth in use.

What does all this 'enable' then?

Pulling all these Enabling Technologies together and looking at the changes over the last ten years, we see these Enabling Technologies coming together in a way that not only redefined the way we communicate and share but one that redefines the fabric of our societies. The speed at which we can communicate, share and develop ideas has reached the point where it is instantaneous.

Many have looked at education and spent much time looking at how to bring about change. Some have looked at technology in education but few have looked at how technology and education interact. One treatise on reforming education was written by Michael Barber. In his 1996 book *The Learning Game: Arguments for an Education Revolution*, Barber looks at how an education system might transform.[1] He wrote the book whilst closely advising Tony Blair on education policy and, subsequently, when Labour came to power in Britain in 1997 Michael played an influential role in the education reform agenda. He led the Standards and Effectiveness Unit (SEU) and was responsible for implementing many reforms. However, despite much investment in technology by that government, the link between technology and effective schools was never made. The potential for technology was identified, but moving to a level of maturity where technology is seen as another tool still appears to be a great challenge.

Twenty years after Michael Barber's book, very little has changed. As I develop this book I will argue that much policy and reform actively mitigated against technology being embedded into high-quality learning.

In the twenty years since Barber wrote his book, technology has developed far beyond that which he was referencing. Reflecting on Barber's writing, it is interesting how closely his thoughts fit with the ideas set out by Andreas Schleicher in the 2015 OECD book on computers and teaching. I will explore that book in more detail later in the book, but in the Foreword to the book Schleicher says 'The impact of technology on educational delivery remains sub-optimal, because we may overestimate the digital skills of both teachers and students, because of naive policy design and implementation strategies.'[2]

To me, Barber and Schleicher make the same point. We are missing the policy frameworks that embed these technology tools into the fabric of learning. We are still so obsessed with the industrial model of learning, Learning Organisations and curriculum that up to now we've missed the fundamental and powerful changes that we need to make to education systems so they remain relevant in this post-industrial information age.

Learning has always happened in the home, around the immediate social environment and between experts in local communities. From storytellers to the local blacksmith, learning was often focused on the passing on of skills that would ensure a productive and fulfilling life. Some argue that the innate ability of people to learn, especially young people, is being submerged under a raft of regulation, testing and benchmarking. The freedom to explore and make connections is being undermined by the very systems that were set up to ensure equity of access to learning.

I am passionate about learning. Giving people the space to explore their understanding of the world around them and play back that understanding is an exciting thing to be part of as an educator. Sharing and working with young people in particular is one of the most rewarding things you can do in my opinion. In 1999, I wrote a book called *The Empowered Citizen – Growing Up in an Information Society* (privately published). In the final paragraph of that book I wrote:

> *I am on the side of the learner because learning is one of the most joyous things you can do. It raises the spirit and spurs you on to more and greater things. Keep looking at the world through the eyes of a learner and you will never grow old in spirit.*

Learning and education

Before I move on I want to think about the words 'learning' and 'education'; they are often used synonymously, but they mean two very different things. We often hear people talk about 'education systems'. Education becomes a descriptor of what society has codified as an accepted set of activities that young people experience between the ages of five and twenty-five. An education system has an agreed curriculum and a broadly agreed approach to how, where and when that curriculum should be delivered. This system has developed over many years and, in most countries, is governed by the political flavour of the day, moderated by tradition and expectation. More often than not, politicians and their advisors who shape education policy have not worked with learners. They are all well-educated, capable of great insight and mostly have a sense of social justice and service at the core of their daily activities. But having not been involved in learning and not worked with young people, you miss something. Reading and studying a topic is never a replacement for experience. Planning and delivering lessons to learners and then marking and feeding back on their work is a unique experience – an experience that brings a different view of learning and, subsequently, of what an education system should strive to deliver.

Learning is what has been going on since the dawn of life, whether it is investigating the natural surroundings or looking for a deeper meaning in the complex world of particle physics. Experimenting and understanding cause and effect is what the human species is good at doing. Exploration of this type rarely, if ever, fits into a regimented working day. When learning is simply defined as knowing a set of facts and rules then we have missed something profound. In an attempt to measure how well an education system performs, are we removing the essence of true learning and replacing it by defining what people know?

As I progress through this book, some questions have driven my narrative. Questions like:

What happens when an industrial model for learning packages up knowledge into bite-sized chunks to be delivered at times that suited that industrial model?

By striving to deliver education to everyone have we unwittingly created a system that stifles the intrinsic ability of the human being to learn and be creative?

Some other observations and thoughts also drive the narrative:

*It appears that some of the underlying social truths that held for many
years are no longer relevant.*
*The rise of the digital revolution of the late 20th and early 21st centuries
has changed things so profoundly that it has left many social systems floundering.*
*Somehow, we have lost the essence of learning that started to be codified
in pre-industrial times when learning was focused on local communities and how that localness drove social cohesion.*
*There are some startling truths about how technology is actually
bringing us back to our pre-industrial roots, with learning able, once
again, to focus on the local community whilst simultaneously being
able to be global.*

As an overarching theme throughout the following chapters I will
always come back to the role of teachers. Those that choose such a
vocation will never be the tech-company billionaires, they will probably
never be the ministers that run regions and countries, but what they will
do is inspire and challenge our young people to be more than they
thought they could be. They will support, nurture and provoke learners
to be as successful as they can and, in doing so, will ensure the social
cohesion that is essential.

Thankfully, our teachers are leading a revolution in our learning
organisations. As we'll see later, teachers naturally understand that
education systems need to reform and transform. However, that transformation and reform process often 'jars' with the absolute need of
society and government to be able to measure outcomes. How do we
measure success if we cannot simply and easily test how many facts an
individual can remember on a given day? How can we measure the
success of an education system if one school is teaching for twenty-five
hours a week whilst another is teaching for thirty-five hours a week?
How can we control the outputs of the education system if the learners
are accessing facts and knowledge outside a sequence that a curriculum
stipulates?

In an industrial model, things need to be ordered. Things need to
happen one after another. To build and deliver goods and services to a
high quality, a strict process must be followed. In that world, it follows
that learning must be similarly organised. One fact must follow

another – there needs to be an agreed progression so that we judge mastery on a simple scale. If a measurement system becomes too complex, comparison becomes impossible; the relative success, or otherwise, of organisations in a system that needs to compare like with like becomes impossible.

Thankfully, there are enough people, organisations and educators who understand how the opposite forces of 'the need to compare performance' and 'the need to provide freedom' can be reconciled; how a system can be shaped to provide both rigour and freedom without the outcomes becoming devalued to a point where they become meaningless. By the end of this book I hope I will have been able to shed some light on those two seemingly opposing views and to have shown where progress and reform is happening and where learning is alive and well.

Finally for this introductory chapter, I would like this book to become a centre for debate and discussion around how we create the bold reforms we need. We must engage the views and ideas of our leading educators because they understand how to make change happen and are grounded in learning. We need to encourage our education thinkers to stand up for the rights of our learners and defend their ideas with cogent and thought-through argument. In our modern era, ideas can travel fast and change can happen quickly.

Notes

1 Barber, M. (1996). *The Learning Game: Arguments for an Education Revolution*. London: Victor Gollancz.
2 Schleicher, A. (2015). *Students, Computers and Learning: Making the Connection*. Paris: PISA, OECD Publishing.

2 Learning never stops

By looking at learning against three ages in history, my intent is not to write a linear history book, although such a task would be simultaneously appealing, daunting and time-consuming whilst also being a worthwhile challenge. What I aim to do is to look at how learning has changed in response to major trends in society. It is clear that the need to learn and the associated education systems that have been created by society follow closely the trends that are being set by local, national and global changes. Rather than spending a lot of time on the historical aspects of the ages, I want to focus on sharing and bringing to light the current trends and help to share ideas and thoughts on how these trends need to be embraced to deliver meaningful education change.

As we look across the landscape of history, we have, at a very high level, moved from learning being centred around the family and the immediate local community, with a focus on apprenticeships and working in a local context, through a massive growth in education systems that culminated in the 1940s with a right for all to have access to education. This led to the creation of industrial-scale Learning Organisations to support the massive increase in the number of learners. Such a development made perfect sense at the time and can be seen as a direct response to the needs that arose out of the Second World War. But it was there that education systems stopped evolving. They ground to a halt in the industrial model whilst society moved on. To make things worse, society is moving away from an industrial model to a more localised, personal and fundamentally agile era. With the rise of technology there is a shift to the localisation of services, but with those services being conceived and delivered on a global scale. Take shopping as an example. Large global corporations that focus on delivering to the individual rather than insisting that the individual goes to large physical shops have emerged. Table 2.1 shares some very high-level thoughts on

Table 2.1 Trends over time

	Pre-industrial	Industrial	Post-industrial
Medicine	Observe Diagnose Treat	Research Understand Document	Monitor Prevent
Music	Live performances	Record	Stream

Learning	Find out what is
	    needed to live
		Teach what
		    we know
			Synthesise
			Collaborate

Retail	Local Immediate	Multiple Global Consumer Stores	Personal Online Delivered Immediate

how various areas of life have changed from the pre-industrial to the current era. As these thoughts and ideas developed, I was intrigued to understand how certain areas of society have developed.

The underlying premise of the table is that the profound changes in society that we have seen over the past 400 years appear to be reinforcing the importance of community. The direction of travel is towards an ever more personal approach. In medicine, we are rapidly moving towards a position where individual patients can monitor and share their personal medical data, through technology, with their physician. As medicine became industrialised with large-scale hospitals, we lost the personal relationship between patient and practitioner. This detailed relationship is beginning to return with the sharing of data. In the world of music, we have gone from music being used in small-scale local gatherings, through an era where large-scale concert halls were constructed, and now to a position where technology can stream into our personal devices any amount of live or recorded music. In retail, we have gone from the local shop, through an era of industrialised shopping centres, to a period when goods are being ordered online and delivered to our home, cutting out the need to go to large shopping centres and making the entire process more personal. But in education we are still steadfastly stuck in the large-scale industrial model – at least when we look at what official policy has to say about what an education system should be. There are many small-scale models where approaches are rapidly changing and opening up new possibilities. In essence, the world is digital, personal and mobile, whilst education systems remain mostly analogue, generic and physically located in one place.

From there to here

What influenced some of the changes during these three ages? As we moved from broadly subsistence-based agrarian systems to an industrial revolution in the 1750s and early 1800s, society changed significantly. Populations grew, towns and cities grew, developed and emerged – the occupations and jobs of the population changed rapidly. Manual labour on the land became labour in factories and the significant migration of populations occurred to meet the demands of the industrial revolution. As society developed again in the late 1990s, the growth of services-based business shifted things once again. As we moved into the early 21st century, the rise of technology and the globalisation of business created a new set of dynamics that have created change and tensions in the very foundation of our society.

What were the key drivers in the past that shaped our world? In the pre-industrial age the agrarian economy dominated but with emerging structures that we would recognise today, but where a rural existence was the norm. Transport was by horse or other beasts of burden and travel took a long time. The industrial revolution saw rapid change, in which steam power provided trains for mass transport and mechanisation transformed the way we lived, consumed goods and communicated. The post-industrial age is an age where the emphasis has moved from the production of goods to the provision of services. Our economy is predominantly driven by services rather than the production and manufacturing of goods, and we talk of technology significantly disrupting the way our society works. Where goods are manufactured, much of the traditional manual labour has been replaced by mechanisation with robotic machines providing what was once achieved by human muscle power.

Change happens…

Change is gradual. Looking back, there are things that make it easier to see the particular elements that defined a new era and it might appear as though change was sudden, but in reality it is gradual. The pace of change is faster now than it was, with the development and adoption of new and popular ideas happening faster than ever. But change is still gradual, even if the rate has increased. And with change comes resistance. The adoption of a new idea or fashion starts with a few people and then grows in popularity. But some resist or deny that the new idea or trend is important. As a student of music, I studied how new ideas in music often met with significant resistance. As composers developed new tonal canvasses they were admired and vilified in equal portions. Critics became split and reviews ranged from the ecstatic to the downright rude. The most striking example was Beethoven. His compositional style started firmly in the classical era, but by the time his Ninth Symphony was complete he had set the course for the Romantic era. But there were those who rejected his Ninth Symphony as being frivolous. History tells us that this work is one of the masterpieces of all time. But the point is that eras and ages overlap; one starts as another is still strongly supported. And the supporters of the status quo have loud and often influential voices. Often leaders and politicians who have invested significant amounts of their time into supporting a particular viewpoint are the slowest to recognise change. Add to this the inevitable turmoil that surrounds change and there is a fertile ground for argument and debate, some of which can take on disturbing tones. And so it is with learning, particularly the age we now find ourselves in. I have a short but interesting book on my shelf called *Understanding Schools as Organizations*.[1] With a foreword by Charles Handy – the author of *The Empty Raincoat* – and the main text by Robert Aitken, the book looks at how schools operate. Despite being published in 1986, it still has relevance today. Their description of a 'federal school' is well worth reading, especially their lamentation at the end of the book that because of the way education is structured the hope for a truly federal system may be impossible to achieve.

Building on the comments I made in the Foreword, education needs to keep up with change, reflect where society is going and seek to remain relevant. Handy and Aitken picked up this challenge thirty years ago and we are still hitting the same issues. In those thirty years, things have got more complicated. Our society has become more globalised, and technology has given us the smartphone and the tablet computer. Our understanding of how people learn has progressed. However, we appear to still be looking to the industrial age to define how, where and when education should be delivered.

Over the next few pages I've developed a little further some of the key trends that shaped the three ages. I would reiterate that this is not meant to be a history book. The aim of focusing on the three ages is to have a view on how learning has been embedded into our society and then use that as a means of examining how our learning systems need to change today and, probably more importantly, how these systems need to keep re-envisioning themselves for the future. This is not a one-off process. The same problems will occur again and again unless we look at how the system needs to be reinterpreted as society changes. Education systems need to be ahead of the game if young people are to have an advantage. The underlying theme of this book is how we integrate technology into our systems now that technology is such an embedded facet of how we live. This is not because I am focusing on technology for its own sake; it is because technology is shaping the society we inhabit. It is fundamentally reforming so much of what we do every day. It is the single biggest trend in the lives of everyone. Education needs to respond to and develop reforms that embrace these social trends.

The pre-industrial age

This very broad categorisation is typically defined by historians as covering everything that occurred before the industrial revolution, which took place between about 1750 and 1850. It was a time before complex machines and tools were developed to perform tasks. It was a time when physical strength and people power made things happen. A time before mechanisation, before steam power and before the widespread rise of literacy and numeracy. A time where formal learning was only accessible to a very few. As a species, we were very good at learning things and made great strides in understanding the way things worked and how to manipulate the world around us.

Whilst writing this book I accompanied our children on a trip to Stonehenge. As I walked round the site, the scale and endeavour of the project really hit home – the skills needed to design and lay out the stone circle, the skills needed to dress the stones to give them a smooth appearance, the skills and organisation needed to bring massive stones from considerable distances and the knowledge of the landscape to ensure that everything was aligned correctly. Not to mention the fact that a large portion is still standing some 5000 years later. It is one of the wonders of the world and a real testament to the ability of the human species to learn, share skills and develop new technology to overcome challenges and difficulties.

As we listen to politicians and policymakers discussing education systems, arguing over the content of a curriculum or getting very

exercised about the nature of when and how often we should test learners, I like to sit back and simply reflect on how successful the human
race has been before we became so obsessed with the nature of the
system. In pre-industrial societies, I don't even think people thought
about learning or education as needing to be anything more than the
passing on of ideas from one generation to another. The nature of the
passing on was done very much 'on the job': learning by doing being one
of the most powerful ways to share ideas, knowledge and to develop both
skills and insight. And in sharing, modifications to processes occurred,
new ideas emerged and systems developed that made things easier,
quicker and more efficient. I do also wonder whether many of the
buildings and monuments we are creating today will still be around and
celebrated in 500 years, yet alone in 5000 years' time.

The industrial age

The industrial age in the west is typically seen as the time after the
industrial revolution of 1750–1850. This age is well documented and
well defined. England led the world through the industrial revolution
– an era where mechanical technology developed quickly and where
mass production became the norm. Following the revolution in
mechanisation and production processes, the industrial age was born.
Changes swept across society, with few areas of life not being touched,
changed or developed in some way as mechanisation rolled across the
world. Agriculture was undergoing significant change as mechanisation enabled new ways of increasing productivity. Agrarian communities were being reshaped as workers who traditionally laboured
in the fields started to migrate to the cities to find alternative work.
Those who made vast fortunes from the industrial revolution began to
have time to think about what a more universal education system
might look like. Wealthy individuals endowed Learning Organisations
and helped to fund and set up wider access to more formal education
organisations.

What was learning like is this era?

I often speak of parents being all too eager to 'outsource' their children's
learning, passing on to others all the responsibilities for learning. And,
in the late 20th and early 21st centuries, governments have been all too

keen to accept this outsourcing challenge. As societies needed to become more productive, parents and guardians needed to 'go to work' – often considerable distances from their homes. As mechanisation enabled greater transport infrastructure, so the opportunity to seek employment away from your immediate community grew. As people worked and travelled further, the family unit was unable to take responsibility for the younger generation whilst they were at work. The pre-industrial model was broken. Work became defined as going to physical locations that were designed to efficiently produce goods or process information using manual labour. This model of going to work has endured, although it is rapidly breaking down. Services-focused organisations created 'offices' where people met and worked together. It made sense, and in the late 20th century the ability to collaborate and communicate with people other than face to face was still extremely limited.

In the industrial age, it made perfect sense to outsource education to experts. As manufacturing processes developed, it became ever more challenging for local craftsmen to make artefacts for a price that was attractive to the growing population. Manufacturing processes also made it possible to produce new artefacts using materials that were previously impossible to work with in a local artisan workshop. Thus, sending young people to places where the education process could be delivered in a cost-effective and measured way was the best way to proceed. The need to educate more people also pushed this model of conformity, regulation and the delivery of an agreed curriculum of content and knowledge so that potential employers could understand what their employees knew and could benchmark their jobs accordingly.

Without much argument, the education system was born. A logical approach was taken and learners were segregated by age and split into conveniently sized groups that settled at between thirty and forty learners in a room with a single teacher. This was efficient and easy to control. It borrowed from models that were already in use in the private school systems and the university system. The system that developed was easy to administer, cost-effective and provided a framework around which governments could start to measure how successful learners were doing as they progressed through the system. Just like in an industrial production process, those that conformed to the specifications were passed through the system and deemed to be successful. Those that did not quite fit or were unable to access the system as well as their peers were judged differently. Very quickly, different kinds of schools were created to ensure that the outcomes were always successful. Thus, a tripartite system emerged in England. To support the system, rigorous testing was put in place that defined how clever someone was – a judgement that often stayed with that individual for the rest of their life, often defined what further education opportunities would be available to them and, from there, what work and career opportunities would be available.

A pioneer in the reform of education systems has described the resultant industrial model as one of 'Cells and Bells'. This description is used to highlight the rather regimented approach to learning, where discrete subjects are taught in discrete spaces for fixed amounts of time. During the work I was involved with in the IBM Reinventing Education project, two colleagues – Dr Jim Schnitz and Dr Janet Azbell – began formulating some ideas around how to summarise the key themes in education systems with reference to how learning is delivered. From working with educators in multiple countries, a summary of these high-level approaches was produced. Table 2.2 presents a view on what we saw in the early 2000s.

The Table 2.2. begins to hint at some of the changes that were occurring in the early 2000s in the way teaching was being delivered. As the industrial age began to be less relevant, the approaches to learning in some small pockets began to develop beyond the well-trusted traditional approaches of a didactic delivery model. The collaborative and independent models outlined in the table begin to codify how the approach to learning could be reformed.

The post-industrial age

Post-industrial societies are commonly defined as the stage in society when the services sector begins to generate more gross domestic product (GDP) than manufacturing. As commented on in more detail later, there is also a definition of post-industrial societies in terms of demographics. The Demographic Transition Model defines a series of phases through which societies pass, the last of which defines a low birth rate and low mortality rate as being typical of a post-industrial age. This occurred in the UK at the start of the 20th century. In the early 2000s, people talked about the *knowledge economy* and the *information society*. These headlines and titles underline the fact that the UK economy was

Table 2.2 Learning and teaching approaches

	Whole class	Groups	Collaborative	Independent
Who teaches?	20–30 students	Teams of teachers work with groups of students. Older students help younger students where appropriate	Teachers, business mentors, parents and other experts are included in the learning process	Students connect with teachers, mentors and peers as needed. Teachers access resources as needed
Where?	Traditional teaching spaces	'Learning spaces' and specialist areas with access to relevant tools/devices and large and small group spaces	The learning environment is extended to work with partner organisations	Learning opportunities accessed from anywhere. Resources are online and teachers and mentors are 'connected' to learners
When?	Traditional lesson approach	In-depth study over longer time frames, crossing traditional subject boundaries	Programmes recognise and provide credit for performance in and out of the school, including work experience	Traditional time patterns need not constrain learning. Enables working with a wider business and community
How?	Face to face in rooms	Interaction with a range of people including industry experts – facilitation predominates	Learning activities include interactions with other participants both physically present and in remote locations	Independent and collaborative team activities are guided by teachers and other mentors as needed. Students become producers as well as consumers of knowledge

developing strongly away from manufacturing and moving towards the creation of *intellectual property*. Manufacturing centres shifted to emerging economies where labour was less costly and where production could, therefore, scale quickly.

The world has changed. The way people work has, and is, changing at a hitherto unmatched pace. The ability to share, communicate and collaborate across borders is now ubiquitous. Any one of us can have an impact at the local, regional, national and global level at the same time. The impact of the individual is not dependent on being in a specific physical place and the ability to share ideas and then travel to any point in the world makes the reach of each of us significantly greater than it ever was.

Elements of Learning Organisations

As with all new ideas and new thinking there is often the need to create a shared vocabulary to aid in discussion and debate. Apparently, the verb 'to Google' is now universally accepted to mean searching the Web. We all know what texting is and we all understand what an app is and how that idea has changed the way we use Smart devices.

To support a discussion around how the post-industrial era has changed and is still changing the nature of Learning Organisations, Table 2.3 lists a series of elements that shape how a Learning Organisation works and operates. I've then commented on how those elements have changed between the industrial and post-industrial era. For the post-industrial era I have listed two models, as we are still in transition. The collaborative model is still quite a challenging and mostly uncommon model. The idea of a system where learners lead the learning is still extreme to many, but extremely powerful when implemented within a secure framework.

I will develop these themes later in the book, particularly when I explore what a 'rebooted' education system might look like. For now, I will leave the Tables 2.2 and 2.3 as a point of reference that I will refer back to in other chapters.

To close this chapter, I would like to sum up as follows: as we exit the industrial era there are things that don't add up in our education systems. Despite clear evidence, our education systems are still pursuing truths that don't make sense in the time we now inhabit. The systems are looking back at the past and not towards the future. We are

Table 2.3 Vision for education systems

Element	Industrial	Post-industrial	
Leadership	Prescriptive	Collegiate	Collaborative – learners often lead
How teachers teach	Teacher as expert	As a facilitator	As a collaborator
How learning happens	Presented by the teacher	Guided by teacher	Through guided discovery and debate
Nature of the curriculum	Subject-based	Faculty-based	Topic-based
How content is organised and presented	Linear	'Manipulate'	Non-linear to support the process of discovery
Physical environment	Classrooms	Flexible spaces based on classrooms	Flexible learning spaces
Visible ICT	Suites of IT	Moveable/portable	Personal
Network design	Client–server	Client–server connected to Internet and Web	Distributed cloud 'everywhere all the time'

wasting the talents of our young people by trying to make their agile and modern thinking fit outdated models. *For complete clarity*, I still support literacy and numeracy as fundamental tenants of any learning system. I support the ethos of self-discipline and the need to know things, but I do not see these as mutually exclusive from the application of technology at the heart of the learning process and of our education systems. I question the need for some approaches to deliver learning when we have devices that can help us recall facts and figures at the push of a button. I especially question approaches when they eat up time in the learning day that means learners do not get time to problem-solve or look at real-world challenges. Simply being able to recall that 9 times 9 is 81 is worthy, but not being able to apply that to a real-world problem that helps you navigate life leaves the learner at a distinct disadvantage. There are places where people have started to make sense of models for the future but these are not mainstream and need exploring and sharing. The biggest challenge in the 21st century is how we shape our education systems to foster agility and creativity, making the most of new tools and technologies in a way that provides for the expansion in human understanding and knowledge that happened in previous ages.

Note

1 Handy, C.B. & Aitken, R. (1986). *Understanding Schools as Organizations.* Harmondsworth: Penguin Books.

3 Education change – it's tough

Many have tried to bring about education change and many have succeeded. In 1944 the largest reform in the history of learning in England was instigated. The Butler Act made significant reforms to the education landscape in England, setting up the tripartite system. That change was a highly significant point in the progress towards trying to build true social equity through education. It was, however, of its time. It is strange then that at the moment, in the early years of the third millennium, we appear to be stuck looking back to this post-war reform for our inspiration for the future. Much of the evidence gathered since the instigation of the tripartite system has shown that the selection processes that the reforms created to manage the flow of learners into schools actually hinder social mobility. Whilst everyone gets an education, the selection process can do more to reinforce social position than it does to create real mobility. This backwards look seems to be born from a fear that if we embrace new ways of working and learning we will somehow lose something essential from our society that the current systems help to reinforce. I'm at a loss to fully understand what it is that we think we will lose, and also at a loss to understand what it is that creates such fear and confrontation between education leaders and policymakers. Literacy is essential, but so is being able to use that literacy to the best possible advantage for the individual. One thing that is clear is that functional literacy as defined in the 1940s has developed considerably and new skills are needed.

Is it that we are on the edge of such a significant change and that the change appears to be so big that the risks also look to be too large to be assessed or managed? Like a magnitude-9 earthquake, is the potential devastation too big to be contemplated and, therefore, being deliberately ignored? In this book, I argue that the risks of ignoring the potential created by the changes are simply too great to be overlooked. We risk slipping further behind other nations and organisations that are embracing the changes that are accelerating every day and giving their systems an advantage.

It appears that change in education is also so mired in political rhetoric that as soon as change and development is discussed or even contemplated, factions take up opposite positions that inevitably lead to confrontation and ill feeling which, in turn, leads to stalemate. Somehow there needs to be a way to set education reform apart from the political process and focus change and development around learning. How to make the system 'apolitical' is perhaps the best way to create lasting reform in this third millennium. However, as long as education is funded by public money then politicians are responsible for the outcomes. Whilst that remains the case, then control over the system, the workforce and investment will stay in the hands of the politicians.

But there are places where, despite all of the above, we are seeing transformation taking place. As I stated earlier, it is happening in small pockets and those pockets are not transferring to the wider system at the moment. In my career, I've been fortunate enough to work as a part of organisations that are creating new models as well as being part of some organisations that have created alternative systems, albeit at a small scale.

Three experiences have shaped my views on education change. The first was my own experience in the classroom, the second was being a programme manager for a group of projects called Reinventing Education for IBM in the late 1990s and the third was working with a highly effective group of academies in and around London during a period of considerable change and upheaval.

Each experience exposed me to learners in very challenging circumstances where often the system was being blamed for their failure. Each experience also brought together extraordinary teams of people who rolled up their sleeves and went about tackling the circumstances of failure to build a better future for individual learners, which then cascaded across wider groups of learners, and each has created a model of how a redefined education system could operate. Maybe there is a clue here about the challenge of reform at the present time. There is not one model that works everywhere; there are multiple models that work in certain circumstances, but that simply do not transfer. In looking at education reform, I have long held a view that simply taking a programme or approach from one circumstance to another rarely, if ever, works. A much more enlightened way is to look at what works in one place and ask, 'How could that work for me?' In asking that question, a dialogue is created that starts to get to the heart of not what someone did, but why they did it. From there a dialogue can continue about what is the same and what is different in each circumstance, and programmes and approaches can be honed to the specific environment.

Three models

Working as a teacher and leader in education is simultaneously the most rewarding and the most challenging job you could ever wish to undertake. Until you've been in the classroom and taught I think it is hard to understand the pressures, challenges and joy that comes from working with learners as they begin to understand the world. Many people see bits of the education system, form an opinion on the profession and often form a view of how it could be done better. There are many facets to teaching, from being an expert in a subject, to managing diverse groups of learners, to planning and marking work, not to mention working with parents and the wider community. The job never ends for the dedicated educator. They think, plan and develop ideas to make the learning better all the time. The profession can be all-embracing and permeate your entire life.

In the classroom

People matter – communities matter

I started my teaching career in 1984 in a 1600-pupil mixed comprehensive school and taught for fifteen years in a variety of Learning Organisations. The first school I taught in was located in a seaside town on the south coast of England. There was a rich diversity of students from a wide range of social and economic backgrounds. Sometimes I think nothing has changed when budgets are being discussed for education. My first classroom was a 1940s 'hut' with oil-fired heaters that periodically filled the room with black soot but never really provided a satisfactory level of warmth. The building was just about watertight, but the wind managed to penetrate the aging structure, making cold winters not the best of times. Before officially starting this job on 1st September, my wife and I volunteered to paint the classroom over the summer holiday. It was in a bit of a state and had not been decorated for a long time. It made for a new beginning for both me and for the aged building. This job marked the start of an exciting five years during which I taught maths and music to large numbers of learners. The school was blessed with a talented and enthusiastic group of staff. Thirty years later their names and faces still stick firmly in my memory. We ran after-school clubs, activities and a wide variety of trips that ranged from local days out to an exchange programme with a school in New Jersey, USA. Despite the challenging circumstances of the area, the people who made the school tick were forward and outward looking. They challenged their students and shaped a variety of experiences that allowed our learners to grow well beyond what the curriculum mandated we should teach.

These people, my colleagues, were focused on unlocking the potential of each individual student. We challenged each other and we challenged the learners. We even did some things that would be considered leading edge today, thirty years later. We managed to find the funds to buy one of the now iconic BBC B microcomputers. It came fully loaded with the excellent BBC BASIC programming language. We worked with our students to write programs and a few of us even wrote our own programs to fill gaps in the curriculum. As a teacher of music and maths, I wrote a simple application that allowed students to put their tunes into the computer as a series of numerical values (great cross-curriculum stuff going on there) and the computer played the music to them. So, we were coding in our spare time, with students working in their own time to find out how these new tools worked. As I mention elsewhere, from the BCC B came the Acorn company that was eventually bought by Apple, became Xemplar and then disappeared.[1] Along the way Acorn also produced RISC OS and RISC PCs.

As I progressed through a fifteen-year career in teaching, I moved to teach IT and was involved with a number of interesting projects including creating a language college and writing the code to create a new network operating system for an early network of computers. Throughout all my years teaching, I recall the colleagues I worked with and the way they focused on unlocking the potential of the learners. They supported each other and cared deeply about the life chances of all their learners.

The learning I take away from my fifteen years in the classroom is that people are the key and the communities they create add value and sustain individuals to perform above and beyond what they thought they could achieve. Whatever the system mandates, dictates or insists, the people in our Learning Organisations will always look beyond the system. They will, if given the chance, support and challenge the learners to broaden their horizons, go beyond their barriers and explore what they can become if self-belief is pursued. Sometimes they will bend the rules to accommodate new ideas and they will go over, around and through barriers that could otherwise be seen as legitimate reasons for giving up. However, real change is hard. In and around education, people argue constantly, put forward counter positions and at times simply refuse to share what they know. In the past, this was maybe understandable because sharing took time and cost money. But in the modern world sharing something is a few taps of a key away. It costs little and happens instantly. In the pre-industrial era sharing was as simple as talking to the person next you. It is only in the industrial era that sharing became cumbersome, complex and time-consuming.

Reinventing Education – well, someone had to!

Change needs a catalyst – everything is not always what it appears to be

In the late 1990s I worked on a programme called Reinventing Education that IBM had initially established in the USA. I answered an advertisement in the *Sunday Times* for an educationalist to support the programme in Europe, the Middle East and Africa (EMEA). When I started out on this adventure little did I know that an initial twelve-month secondment would be extended to eighteen months and then move into a permanent job role within this global giant of a corporation. That started a journey that opened my mind to education systems across the world. I met with leading education thinkers, policymakers and researchers. The cultural mix and breadth of experience has given me ideas and insights that, to this day, still set my mind racing. More of that later.

The Reinventing Education Programme was funded with $75 million from IBM's community relations budget. This was philanthropic money that IBM reinvested into community programmes. The company had always been very involved in supporting local community projects in the USA where the company had a major presence, and education had featured as a focus with many small but unconnected projects. Although seen as a technology company, IBM also helped organisations make change happen. The very fact that technology was bringing about many of the changes organisations were struggling with made it even more important to support and understand change.

The programme was born in 1997 and was created and supported by IBM's chief executive officer (CEO) Lou Gerstner. Gerstner was brought into IBM in 1994 to effectively save the company from being broken up into separate units. He took over the leadership mantle at a time when IBM was on its knees. His subsequent turning around of the company is now a business school case study. As well as turning the company around, Gerstner turned his attention to bringing cohesion to the community relations work that IBM was involved in within all 169 countries where it operated. The Reinventing Education Programme was born as a response to the significant issues that beset a wide range of school districts across the USA. Gerstner saw an opportunity to bring the power of IBM into the heart of communities across the USA and in the other countries in which it operated. He also had a history of supporting education programmes from his time in Amex and Nabisco. To this day, his foundation continues to support education projects.

Initially, the Reinventing Education Programme focused on school districts in the USA, where reform was being actively sought by the senior leaders and the local communities. The recipe was simple. Districts were invited to present a proposal for up to $2 million of funding to help tackle a significant issue. The district was expected to match the grant using staff and other resources. Whilst IBM was seen predominantly as an IT company, the grant programme did not focus on giving away technology. It went deeper than that. It focused on supporting what the programme called systemic change. The aim of the programme was to look at processes and the way schools worked, and to help them re-engineer these core underlying processes using technology as the catalyst. The programme involved researchers from the world-renowned IBM research community, experienced professionals, educators and those skilled in working alongside communities to support change. The programme was reviewed by Harvard Professor Rosabeth Moss Kanter in 1999. She wrote a short piece called 'From Spare Change to Real Change'[2] that looked at how well-targeted philanthropic investment can create models for significant and lasting change in society.

Once the programme had worked across a significant number of sites in the USA it was expanded to become a global programme. As we worked across these various sites it became clear that many education systems were not providing what learners needed or wanted. The complexities of why were many, but we started supporting those we worked with to make system-wide changes that were then used as exemplars for others to review and understand. The programme attracted some attention, but because it was not giving away lots of shiny new computers the press was more subdued than about many other corporate philanthropic programmes where free technology was the focus. I believe the outcomes and learning from the programme were very significant. It looked at deep-seated issues around processes and organisations and asked serious questions about how technology could work to improve processes. In effect, it looked at the 'back office' systems and sought to reform those to make change deep-seated. The change being sought was improved outcomes. Most other such programmes look at what I would call the 'front office' and focused on giving new laptops, tablets or software to young learners. Whilst this is attention-grabbing and gets news coverage, it appears to do little to improve or even change the way learning happens. At best, it gives some impetus to certain kinds of learners; at worst, the devices completely disrupt the prevailing teacher-led pedagogical mode. The end results are disappointing at best and damaging at worst. In 2004 an independent evaluation was carried out of the Reinventing Education Programme by the Centre for Children and Technology. Their evaluation noted that technology was only part of the solution at the grant sites. They noted that alongside the technology, human change had to take place. They also commented that technology was a catalyst for changes in communication.

The learning I take from this experience is that education reforms need to look deeply and widely at what needs to be re-engineered. Simply tinkering at the edges is not enough. As in 1944 with the work of Butler, there are times in history when nothing less than a radical change programme will set a new course. We are at such a point in history now. There are a lot of new ideas around. The edtech investment sector is booming, with a new idea emerging nearly every day. How many of these ideas will last more than a few years and make a significant impact only history will show. However, we need catalysts to make change happen or to increase the pace of change. With the Reinventing Education Programme, technology was mostly just that – a catalyst for change. The changes it brought about made people look at processes that had been taken for granted for many years. By looking at those process and structures, a dialogue was started about how to make change happen that was positive and benefited the learners.

There are significant and fundamental things that have to change in our education systems and we need to set out a new agenda for education and learning that looks forward and embraces the possibilities of our current age. Just as we did in the industrial age, we need to look deeply and profoundly at what is driving society and then reconceptualise our education systems around those drivers. Technology is, of course, a driver, but it is also just a tool. I would suggest that the real driver is our ability as a species to find things out faster, share things faster and work collaboratively as never before. Technology is just the enabler, a tool we have invented to support us on our quest for understanding and knowledge. In the final chapter, I will set out how I think we can leverage these changes and provide a blueprint for a 'rebooted' education system.

Chains, families and groups

When are we one and when are we many? The power of collaboration

When I think of Learning Organisations, many of which have an identical purpose in serving their communities and many of which work within a few miles, often less, of each other, it appears to make sense that they should share and work very closely together. In England, we can argue that for decades this has indeed been the case, with various structures in place to aid organisations to work with each other. Some of these structures have been formal, like local education authorities, and some have been voluntary. At the political end of the spectrum, the local authority (LA) route sought to group organisations together by geography, which made sense on some levels but created challenges on others. However, I think we need to look a bit deeper into the systems and unpick some of the barriers that have emerged that make many of the current models not fit for purpose.

In 2014, I co-authored a report called 'Technology in Education: A System View'.[3] There were many things that intrigued me about the work we did for this report, but the thing that has stood out the most since the report was launched was the way our Learning Organisations in England are overseen at government level. If we look at learning from aged three to twenty-three we will cover the journey that most people make as they move from early childhood to being adults. Learning is roughly split up as follows (I say roughly, as there is a wide degree of variation):

Between three and five years old you are eligible to attend nursery school, from five to ten years old you attend primary school and from eleven to sixteen years old you attend secondary school. At sixteen you can stay at school or move to a post-16 college, and from there you can go to university when you reach eighteen years of age. The system varies. If you opt for a private education then you go through a pre-prep and prep school model, moving at eight and thirteen, and then on to a 'public school' where you can stay until you are eighteen. Some schools offer all-through provision where you can stay until you are eighteen. It is not surprising that some people find it very confusing. To add to the mix, we have introduced city technology colleges (now mostly converted to academies), academies, free schools, university technical colleges, studio schools, space schools and other models into the mix in order to create and provide a wide range of local choice. On the whole, university is a much simpler model. Most organisations providing education from eighteen years and upwards have become universities and offer broadly the same three- or four-year degree options, with Masters and PhD options available for further study. You will recall that I have chosen 'Learning Organisation' as a general term to avoid creating confusion over any of the many models.

If we look at where these various stages of learning get their direction from, then a similarly confusing model emerges. Organisations that provide education up to the age of sixteen get their guidance under law from the Department for Education (DfE). If you are a 'school' that also has provision for sixteen- to eighteen-year-old learners, then you still broadly get guidance from the DfE. However, if you are a stand-alone college that provides for learners from sixteen to eighteen, then you get guidance from the Department for Business, Innovation and Skills, and if you are running a university you have a separate minister who provides guidance. Funding then becomes ever more complex. Schools that work under a LA get funding via the LA, with funding held back by the LA for aggregated services. If, however, you are an academy, a free school or another kind of new start-up school you will get your funding directly from the government with no holdback. If you are part of an academy chain there will be a master funding agreement in place between the chain and the government and your funding will come via that route. Confused? If we examine the curriculum then we find that we have a national curriculum that all maintained schools should follow; however, this does not apply to academies or free schools (and the other types of new schools) and has never applied to private schools. All of this is a complex web of connections and interconnections. The bottom line is that I believe the whole rationale for working together has been lost in this complex web of connections, funding models and links with various government departments. We need a fundamental reform to bring simplicity and clarity to the system. We need clarity in how the government provides advice and this clarity needs to be linked to funding, it needs to be unambiguous and it needs to take into account the journey that learners take through the system. Whilst I have described the system in England, the work that I have done internationally shows that similar complex systems exist in most countries and regions. Upon analysis, the complexity looks ludicrous, but it is just a result of the way education systems have developed over time and is not untypical of many public services.

I've been fortunate to work for and with a wide range of organisations in my career. I worked in a school that was one of the first to opt out of LA control and get its budget directly from government. I have worked in the independent education sector where fees were collected and I also worked for a chain of academies that grew rapidly and now support many schools across South London. That job allowed me to also work closely with colleagues from other groups and chains of academies. In addition, I most recently worked for a UK small and medium-sized enterprise (SME) that supplied services to education organisations. Therefore, I think I have a unique view of this broad spectrum of models and how they impacted on learner outcomes.

When I look across the various models, I'm struck by the progress being made in some academy groups. Without carrying out a very large-scale and deep analysis, I note that the organisations that are progressing the fastest are those that are being driven by business leaders who are, or who have been, significant entrepreneurs, and by those with a particular view of how to do things differently. These business leaders instinctively know that the status quo, whilst important, rarely drives new ideas and innovation. These leaders also know that working by the rules is important but so is being in the middle of the debate to help develop and transform the rules for the good of the wider system. At this inter-section of business and education lies a deep vein of significant opportunity. The education system provides stability and a laser-sharp focus on standards, whilst the entrepreneurial spirit asks significant questions about how things can be done differently and how circum-stances can be tackled to create success for everyone, not just those from advantaged backgrounds. The entrepreneur also knows that being different is important. By being different new opportunities can open up that others can miss. But above all they appear to really understand what it means to share ideas across an organisation. They instinctively know when to leave organisations alone and when working together will drive up standards across the group.

The best of these chains does not try to impose working method-ologies on their members but they do stop similar organisations from making the same mistakes as others have done. They avoid repetition of errors and rapidly share success, thus driving forward improve-ment. They have operational models that they know work well and suggest these are used unless something more compelling can be presented. When organisations that are not performing at the highest level join a group, they are not left alone to drift forwards; they are welcomed into the chain and offered support and advice that will drive up outcomes. Nothing is left untouched, from the relatively straight-forward areas of building maintenance to the more complex areas of staff performance. Where things are not working they are tackled head-on and swiftly addressed by providing support and ideas from similar experiences. At the centre of what they do are the learners – they are the focus for all activities. However radical or uncomfortable the change needed, it is always made to improve the outcomes for the learners. Sharing ideas and experience works, and it works well, but above all it has to be about learning and the outcomes. Simply talking for the sake of talking is a waste of time. As is needless 'education tourism' where people get together for a cosy chat about some broadly defined ideas.

There are also other models that are making significant differences in a broad context. They are taking the widest possible view on what it means to deliver learning in the local context within which they operate. As I will explore later, these organisations are looking beyond just education. They are building a network of social change by looking at Learning Organisations alongside other social services like healthcare, housing and youth and community work. The people driving these organisations are looking at what it takes to bring about a revolution in what it means to learn.

Three into one

If I pull together the learning approaches from the three examples, I see one clear thread emerging – the focus on the learner. The focus on how to make a system work for the learner becomes paramount, not making the learner fit into the system. If something does not work then it needs to be changed. The change must not be arbitrary but must be focused on reforming the system for the good of the learner. The agents for this change are, I believe, also clear. There are three: 1) the teachers and associated professionals who care deeply about the learners and their life chances. I include here leaders. Without high-quality leaders and teachers, nothing changes. 2) Technology and the possibilities it creates to examine processes and systems: from being able to email ideas around rapidly to relatively complex technology solutions that can redefine processes and systems. 3) The way teachers update and improve their skills. This professional development for education has long been delivered in ways that are not making the most of the opportunities working together should offer. Mass training of teachers is not the best way of improving the learning experience. Research and practical observation has time and again shown that getting teachers together to share expertise and debate approaches works best. The industrial training model of putting everyone in a room and telling them how something works simply fails to get across the subtleties and complexities of pedagogy. Sharing ideas, preferably in the classroom and working with high-quality pedagogues, creates powerful ways of sharing how to improve the learning process. Technology also supports high-quality teachers to deliver ever more inspiring and interesting lessons. If learning is about nothing more, it is about igniting a spark of curiosity in someone that leads to an exploration of new ideas and ends up with learning.

The technology myth

Within the context of reforming education, technology is essential in this post-industrial age. Technology need not be complex. It need not be expensive, it need not be beyond the skills of everyone to utilise it for the good of learning. Too much mystique is created around technology to the point of distraction and to the point that technology becomes an obsession that takes time away from the important areas for debate. Technology just needs to work, each time and every time it is called upon within a learning environment. If you are working as part of a chain of schools, why does each school in the chain need different technology? Standardise on a basic configuration and roll that out. You will save time and money, and support teachers and leaders to be more effective. In the post-industrial era, we need to see technology as a tool that supports great learning. Great teachers are embracing it to do everything from delivering lessons to sharing ideas via social media (more of this in later chapters, but in all that we do and think we must not overcomplicate what is just another tool). Please, take away the myths, stop making it something that is difficult and stop making a separate case for technology in education.

'Difficult to manage but impossible to resist'[4]

As a final section to this chapter I am reminded of something that Diana Oblinger said. I met Diana a couple of times when she was involved in the IBM Reinventing Education Programme. I doubt she would remember me but I recall her talking passionately about the potential for technology to support better learning. Her passion was born from practical experience and based on observations of how engaged learners had become in previously complex subjects and ideas when technology had been added to the mix of teaching and learning tools. In a short article, way back in 1999, Diana talked about the potential for technology in education and the way it was going to change the entire fabric of learning. It was in that article that she commented that technology in education was going to be *'difficult to manage but impossible to resist'*. I think her words are well crafted. Many who are yet to really understand the role of technology in 21st-century learning cannot themselves resist the lure of using the technology to improve their personal productivity. They also find it hard to resist requests from fellow educators to invest in these tools and resources that in some way delight and inspire learners of all ages.

Partly as a response to this thought from Diana that has stuck with me all these years, and partly in response to working with many organisations that are working hard to understand how they implement technology,

I created what I call an Education Digital Maturity Index (EDMI). The six elements of the 'index' ask questions about how ready an organisation is to add technology to their mix of tools. I've copied in the index below:

EDMI

1   **Digitally mature leaders** – How do leaders use technology? How do they encourage others to use technology? Is the use of technology fully embedded into their vision for the organisation? How does their vision for technology support enhanced outcomes?

2   **Digitally mature teachers** – Are teachers confident about using technology? Do they have technology embedded into their pedagogical practice? Do teachers share their great practices between each other? Do teachers use technology to teach and work across areas of knowledge?

3   **Digitally mature students** – We usually think of students as the masters of technology, but often they need as much support as everyone else. Are all students confident in using technology? Are all students able to access and use technology? Does the use of technology support students to perform better?

4   **Digitally relevant curriculum** – Without a review of the curriculum, technology can often not be fully exploited. Have leaders and teachers reviewed the curriculum to ensure that technology is being used effectively? Have curriculum activities been specifically designed to make effective use of what technology can offer? Will the curriculum take advantage of the opportunities for broader learning? Continued professional development (CPD) is embedded here as a prerequisite for delivering great learning.

5   **Robust and well-designed infrastructure** – Has the infrastructure been designed to support the multiple personal devices that might be deployed? Has the connectivity been checked to see if it is sufficient? Has the active network infrastructure been configured to support the data it will need to process? Has the wireless infrastructure been designed to support the device strategy?

6   **Classrooms and space** – An understanding of how classroom spaces, buildings and campuses support the use of technology – traditional classrooms and ICT suites support certain types of technology. What happens when you suddenly introduce mobile

devices? Are traditional learning spaces suitable for mobile personal learning? Do classrooms have the spaces and facilities to make mobile learning successful?

Without a review of all the areas outlined above I do not think that technology can be effectively embedded into a Learning Organisation. It can be added around the edges, with areas of great practice made possible and where individuals can flourish in specific areas, but there will not be a systematic embedding of technology so that everyone uses it at appropriate times and places and such that the organisation fundamentally transforms. I've outlined my ideas of a fully transformed system in the final chapter and this concept of digital maturity features again there as part of the wider system.

Evolution that brings about a revolution

Change for the sake of it is of no use and needs to be avoided; looking constantly at how we can develop and evolve systems is, however, essential. In 1913, Henry Ford fundamentally changed the way production lines operated by looking at how to reinterpret the way production was carried out. In turn, this became the 'just-in-time' system that was comprehensively implemented by Toyota. In the early 1990s, James Dyson reimagined the way that vacuum cleaners should work and created dual-cyclone machines. And so, we can go on looking at examples of where approaches to problems have been reimagined, leading to ideas and processes that move us forward and allow us to make the most of changes in the way things work and operate. It is this level of inventiveness that needs to be addressed for our education system. One thing that is clear – it is going to be hard to create the necessary change without getting embroiled in the politics and rhetoric that always accompanies this kind of deep thinking about education. I am clear, however, that what we need is rapid evolution that eventually brings about a revolution in how we think and talk about education systems.

Notes

1 Wikipedia. (2006). Acorn Computers. Available at: http://en.wikipedia.org/ wiki/Acorn_Computers [2017].

2 Moss Kanter, R. (1999). From Small Change to Real Change. Available at: https://hbr.org/1999/05/from-spare-change-to-real-change-the-social-sector-as-beta-site-for-business-innovation [2017].

3 Penny, J. et al. (2014). Technology in Education: A System View. Available at: www.ednfoundation.org/wp-content/uploads/TechnologyEducation_systemview.pdf [2014].

4 Oblinger, D. & Verville, A.-L. (1999). Information Technology as a Change Agent. Available at: https://library.educause.edu/resources/1999/1/information-technology-as-a-change-agent [2017].

4 The new social truths

In Chapter 1 I mentioned that some of the things that have underpinned our societies for many years are rapidly changing. There are some trivial examples and some more profound. In general, our societies are becoming less formal and more forgiving of informality. The young have always been less formal in working together than older generations. Some see this demise of formality as some kind of indication that respect or manners are being degraded. Taboo subjects that were not spoken about are now regularly discussed. From sexuality to drug abuse, the focus is now to discuss these topics to provide information and ensure that decisions are made based on fact and not on rumour or false ideas. Things have changed dramatically in the last twenty years. When I started teaching in the mid-1980s we were only just beginning to explore how we should talk about sex education in the classroom and, likewise, with topics around drug abuse. Now these topics are embedded into the mainstream of education practice. More recently there has been an ever more open and frank discussion about mental health. This is undoubtedly a good thing. The taboos and secrecy that surround mental health are being eroded.

In England, the policy to allow parents and other groups to open new free schools has received a varied response, mostly based on political persuasion. Each group wishing to open a school creates a detailed set of documentation for review and are then subject to public tender for the various services they will need to run their school. They are each given a budget to spend on technology and each group shares their education vision. Having read a large number of the tender documents, I was struck by recurring themes around creating new learning environments; environments where collaboration and communication facilitated by technology were essential elements. At times, these visions were at odds with the guidance issued by the authorities, but they were still pursued with considerable vigour and conviction by the groups setting up the organisations. These people were, on the whole, speaking on behalf of their communities and were articulating new models for learning.

In the following pages, I've reflected on how some new truths are emerging in our society that should make us stop and think very carefully about how we shape education systems for the future.

New truth #1: learning has become social (again)

In our three ages of learning we have seen a dramatic shift in how, where and when learning takes place. In pre-industrial times learning was very much a social exercise for all but a few who chose the path to scholarship via the church or via the relatively few elite Learning Organisations that cost a considerable amount to attend. For the vast majority of people, learning took place as part of what we would define today as apprenticeships or was part of their everyday life. In an agrarian society, working alongside a parent or community member allowed an individual to gain the skills and knowledge they needed to survive. By working collaboratively, early societies learnt to work towards shared and agreed goals. I once saw literacy defined as '*what you need to survive in your society*'. This statement very much contextualises literacy to your society rather than abstracting it into a narrower definition of literacy. Quantifying literacy is challenging. The definition of what literacy is becomes demanding. There are some excellent books and text on this, but a short paper by Devon Lemire gives a very useful background and summary of some of the challenges.[1]

Before universal education for all, young learners were expected to work within the social context of a business or an organisation to gain their skills and knowledge. They were part of the community and acquired their knowledge and skills by working alongside an experienced craftsman, skilled person or knowledgeable individual. Thus, apprenticeships were born. The history of apprenticeships could fill a separate book. However, the fundamental premise of an apprenticeships approach to learning is that you are rooted in providing what people want and can makes changes and develop very quickly. So, from the beginning of time learning has been a social activity based around learning a skill or acquiring knowledge. In the industrial age, we lost the social nature of learning. By creating efficient and large-scale buildings where learning happened, we started to take learning away from the social roots that nourished it. As we became better at implementing this industrial-scale learning it became necessary to develop a list of the things people needed to know. We no longer had the contemporary experience of directly seeing what was needed as we worked alongside the expert practitioner. Thus, a curriculum was born, which over time became an abstracted version of the knowledge needed to become proficient at activities and function in society. By the very nature of the exercise the curriculum becomes ever so slightly removed from the reality of the jobs being done by the experienced practitioner until we end up with a curriculum that is significantly removed from the reality of life. The dislocation is gradual – like navigating wherein a one-degree drift off course is initially trivial but, over time, takes you well off course.

And so we are, with education systems, navigating gently off course with the degree of drift not seen as significant until we suddenly realise that we have lost sight of the very reason we were engaging in the education system in the first place. I do believe in knowledge for its own sake and in the purity of learning, but not at the expense of a lack of being able to function in society. If a curriculum teaches things that are no longer of any use or that have become out of date then the education system has failed, regardless of whether or not the learner can recite and reproduce out-of-date facts and ideas. However good a Learning Organisation is at teaching, if the things it teaches are of no use then it must be failing the users of the organisation.

With the social media tools we have at our fingertips, embedded as they are into our Smart devices, we can be inherently social once again. Whether it is keeping in touch with family members as we travel around, talking to friends or working with colleagues thousands of miles away, the ability to be social with each other is now ubiquitous. It appears strange to me that this great opportunity to share and collaborate has been met with such negativity in education. So many Learning Organisations ban the use of these tools. The often-quoted rationale for this ban fails to make sense beyond the need for a command-control structure to exist. As we rapidly move away from the industrial model we move (back) into a very social world. This time, however, our social context is set at a local, national *and* global level. I can just as easily exchange ideas with someone one street away as I can with someone on a different continent. One of the arguments about our industrial learning model is that we need our learners to socialise and that can only happen in these gigantic buildings where many hundreds of unrelated people are forced together for a few hours each day for an average of forty weeks a year. Working with a variety of people is a skill but that skill is not going to be exclusively gained in the Learning Organisation. What we do is help and guide the socialisation that takes place in these environments and therein lies an important point. I commented elsewhere that in the mid-1980s we were just starting to realise that we needed to engage in learning experiences with young people around sex and drug education. Simply ignoring the subject was not helping; it was, in fact, allowing myths to promulgate and for disinformation to take hold. So why are we treating digital social tools, mobile devices and technology in the same way?

Countless Learning Organisations still ban the use of personal mobile devices, insisting that they are left in bags and turned off. These are the same devices that could be used for great learning. We should be embracing these devices, talking with and helping learners to understand how to avoid being coerced into doing potentially harmful things with the devices. The mantra should be: '*devices on the table, screens up and let's see what you've been doing on the device*'. This approach can help to highlight any potentially harmful practices, lets us share strategies with learners on how to avoid potentially damaging situations and starts to allow us to model powerful strategies for using our devices to learn. As I stressed earlier, this is not a comment on the device. It is a comment on how education should be preparing learners for the world they will inhabit. Just as the printing press democratised the distribution of books and arguably led to an explosion of literacy, so these new tools are leading to an explosion in how we share and communicate.

One of the key questions that emerges is: where do the boundaries lie between socialising and learning? The fear is that social software and personal devices allow learners to engage in subversive activities that somehow undermine the fabric of the Learning Organisation. If we cast the Learning Organisation in such a way that using these tools is not supported then we create the very situation we seek to avoid. Learning just got a lot more social . . . or got back to being a lot more social. We'd

E-Safety.

better understand that new social truth and design our organisations accordingly (see truth #3).

New truth #2: IT became ICT

We have had IT for many years. IT was taken as a definition for hardware and software systems on physical machines that sat in offices and then latterly in Learning Organisations. The devices became linked together in networks called local area networks (LANs) and data was shared between machines using a client–server architecture. Give data a context and you end up with information. This paradigm would have happily continued if military and university researchers has not seen the potential of interconnecting these LANs, initially using telephony infrastructure, to create wide area networks (WANs). Add to this the creation of email and all of sudden you could communicate using the IT, so we had the 'C' added to make ICT. There is no standard definition for ICT because it means many things to many people, but by inserting the 'C' we recognised the significance of technology to support communication. As networks developed and mobility took hold, the 'C' became the greater focus for the use of IT.

But I believe that this is about more than just the technology. Yes, it enables ways of sharing that we have only dreamt about, but it also facilitates what people like to do best – talking, exchanging ideas and working together to create new ideas. Since the start of time we have been sharing ideas and have developed complex language structures to allow us to share ever more complex thoughts and ideas. In all of our three ages the ability to communicate and share ideas has been essential to development. So why all of a sudden has being able to share more often and more quickly become such a bad thing? As an educator, I want to know as soon as possible if my learners are stuck on something so that I can provide help and assistance. As well as better communication, this technology revolution also gives us access to previously unthinkable amounts of knowledge, opinion and conjecture. Even ordering a book on a subject is just a click away rather than a potentially lengthy trip to a shop or a library. By the way, don't stop going to the bookshop or the library! Whilst you can order, buy and have delivered to your door any book you can think of, the trip to the bookstore or to the library will expose you to books that you never knew existed and browsing the shelves might just bring you to something new and exciting. Our modern digital repositories are extensions of the traditional library. Using these tools, we can share our insights and understanding, and we can synthesise ideas to create new ideas and thoughts, find new insights into how things work and meet new colleagues to work with and collaborate with in the future. Learning was always social, as explored in truth #1, and now we are able to extend that 'socialness' and even enable new 'socialness' in ways defined and supported by the new tools we have created.

If we thought that we could ignore the 'C' then we only have to look at the number of social devices. There are platforms for collaboration that are replacing traditional software approaches. The Google ecosystem based on Google Chrome and Android, or Office 365 based on the Windows platform are both built for collaboration and communication. The Apple ecosystem also enables the seamless sharing of ideas, pictures and documents as a core function of the operating system. The use of a particular collaboration platform, like Office 365 or Google Apps, does not necessarily dictate the underlying operating system because apps exist that work across the major operating systems. There is no single ecosystem that dominates the world of work. Whilst there are claimed to be 1.25 billion computers with Windows installed (figures from Microsoft Worldwide Conference), there are equally, as I write, 4.8 billion unique mobile subscribers with 7.9 billion devices (see www. gsmaintelligence.com). These connections and devices are running the three major mobile operating systems from Google, Apple and Microsoft. As I write, market data tells us that the Android mobile OS has a 62% share of the market with Apple iOS devices having a 28% share. The remaining 10% is split between Microsoft at 4% and Blackberry with a diminishing share of the market. The latest data is available at www.netmarketshare.com.[2]

Further research of these figures shows that Android dominates in emerging markets as the OS is free, making the cost of a device considerably less than Apple iOS or Windows-based devices. Notwithstanding the economic argument, the compelling story is that there is no single dominant operating system any more, the picture is more complex and subtle – our young learners will inhabit a world where they will need to move between ecosystems and devices. Our Learning Organisations need to reflect this diversity within a well-managed overall solution approach. In effect, the use of devices is transcending the *exposure to various devices & software*

45

operating system. As we become ever more familiar with the way devices work then the underlying technical architecture and operating system become less important to the end user. The dominance of touch interfaces and the simple use of gestures makes accessing features and software functions simple and intuitive. As the use of voice commands becomes ever more popular and accurate, the way we access technology will become ever more intuitive.

There is still a delineation between using ICT for what I'll call 'socialness' and the use of ICT for research. Society still tends to see using technology for socialness as being rather frivolous and not of any significance. This leads to these technologies not being taken seriously in most Learning Organisations and is, I believe, fuelling the usage patterns we see rather than creating positive models for how these technologies can be leveraged for better learning. Many of our Learning Organisations are not structured to support or make the most of these tools, still being grounded in physical organisational structures that mitigate against using social media for anything serious. When we see education talking about communications technology we tend to hear a set of well-rehearsed comments and phrases that often set minds racing and instil fear into society. The focus is on the negative and rarely on the positive. Many of the things we read about do not accurately reflect what is going on. I've written about this in more detail in Chapter 7.

My hope is that as we move education systems forward the potential for communication and collaboration systems will emerge. As the number of devices continues to grow and as education takes charge of and even creates social networking sites, then the potential will finally be seen. The contemporary nature of shared learning experiences will be seen as powerful and be used by all educators. I've long said that the device revolution is only the start; it's what we can learn about how people are learning, when people learning and what they learn that will be critical. The ability to share real-time data about what you are doing is a real opportunity to make a step change to how Learning Organisations are run.

I have one final observation to make about the 'C' in ICT. If you want to communicate and share then we need places where we can safely share ideas and content. There is still considerable mistrust in the locations that some of the global IT companies are using to store data. This storing and sharing needs to become more local and more under the control of individuals. This will happen as systems develop and become more intelligent – it is an inevitable consequence of the artificial intelligence (AI) work that is currently occupying some of our finest researchers. My hope is that it will become very easy for educators to create, manage and shape spaces to store and share digital assets. Some may argue that this is already simple, but it does currently take a degree of understanding to make the systems behave as you want them to. For serious, group-based collaboration and sharing, ingenious solutions are required. As people work together, 'stuff' emerges – like noisy chatter in a room – and it needs to be stored and made sense of by our machines and not just by humans. How do we create this consensus from all the chatter? The solution is imminent and in the next five years it will be with us in serious and usable ways. Big Data work is currently taking place that can spot trends and patterns and make sense of large data sets. When we apply this to learning then the 'C' will be essential. What we will see is value being derived from synthesis as well as from original ideas.

New truth #3: learning spaces and learning places are everywhere

With the maturity of technology comes the breaking down of the requirement for our industrial-scale learning buildings. Economies of scale shift when learners can access what they need, when and where they need it. This all sounds radical and fanciful because we still have firmly in our minds the learning model of a curriculum being delivered by a group of experts. We still see the need for teachers, as they are now, working within these industrial-scale facilities. The new social truth is that learning is happening in a wide variety of places that we would not traditionally think of as Learning Organisations.

In 1999, I wrote a series of essays that were informally circulated to a number of government and industry sources. The collection was titled 'The Empowered Citizen – Growing Up in an Information Society' and I spoke of a learning revolution supported by technology that would see students studying as their guardians shopped. This has happened. We are also seeing an explosion of online Learning Organisations that provide a range of experiences that support learning on devices that were only ever developed for communication. The new truth is that learning is no longer tied to a specific physical environment. The notebook and pencil liberated learners to leave their desks and start to document the world, relying on skilful sketches to illustrate what they saw. That has developed into using digital images and digital annotation. These digital annotations take place in any location, at any time and record in more detail than was ever possible before. You don't need to have the skills of Leonardo da Vinci to capture what you see as you travel.

This does not immediately mean that we will see the wholesale dismantling of physical learning buildings, but we will see the gradual demise of these buildings in their current form. We will see smaller and even more local learning hubs. These can be created in nearly any building, as I have commented elsewhere – anything from a 'pop-up' school to the reuse of other surplus buildings. The expensively designed buildings we currently see being built will remain, their use and purpose transitioning over time. As we begin to understand that we need to measure our experiences as well as outcomes – 'how' we have learnt as well as just 'what' we have learnt – we will see that physical locations, whilst important, are no longer the focus. Some of the most successful learning models that exist do so by recognising that learning is about being social and socialness needs interaction. Interaction means communicating in some form, communication needs facilitation and that facilitation can and needs to take place in a wide variety of locations. Our new learning spaces need to be at the centre of communities in a way they have never been before and they need to support multiple interactions between learners and the wider community both locally and internationally. Ideas do not stick to borders and neither do our learners. Over the past two years I have seen multiple applications for new schools courtesy of the 'free schools revolution' in England. Many of these new organisations talk of a shift to project-based learning where the more traditional learning space design is dismantled in favour or spaces that are configurable. The revolution has started, it is happening and cannot be stopped.

New truth #4: 'difficult to manage but impossible to resist'[4]

I referenced this quote earlier, but I would like to develop that thinking a bit further. In a short article written way back in 1999, Diana Oblinger talked about the potential for technology in education and the way it was going to change the entire fabric of learning. In that article, she commented that technology in education was going to be *'difficult to manage but impossible to resist'*. I think her words are well crafted.

Many who are yet to really understand the role of technology in 21st-century learning are regularly using the very same technology to improve their personal productivity. Whilst presenting to a group of head teachers in mid-2016, I commented that they had all been using their devices as I presented. I just happened to be presenting as the British Government was undergoing a reshuffle of ministers and the Education Department was being reshaped as I spoke. Naturally, being educators, they were all very keen to see who would get what job in the reshaped department.

This is the new social truth. We are all at it . . . using our technology for everything all the time. Even those who speak against the use of technology in learning are using the technology themselves to communicate with colleagues, family and friends. They might not yet have made the leap from personal use to use in their organisation but they see the potential and probably can't function without it themselves. In this way, Diana had it spot on; 'difficult to manage' is the critical phrase here. But why is it difficult to manage? Probably because these end users are trying to make the technology fit the current models of learning. Andreas Schleicher[3] talks of not embracing 21st-century pedagogies, but what are 21st-century pedagogies? Who is defining them and are they being taken seriously by those that run our education systems? Sometimes I think it is like the arguments that were put forward when calculators were becoming readily accessible. Those with an expertise in mental arithmetic were able to beat the calculator, but when the calculations become more complex then the device overtakes even the best mental mathematician just as the car overtakes even the fastest runner. Whilst running fast is still seen as a fantastic achievement very few of us would don our running shoes for a journey of tens of miles – instead, we jump on some form of mechanical transport.

Why should technology be so hard to manage? Do we mean the physical management of hardware and software or do we mean the processes that are required to effectively use the hardware and software? We probably mean both. Whilst current education systems do not measure how well we collaborate or communicate, the facilities to do those two things don't feature in a heavily tested world. When we are not testing the process by which we learn something and only the outcome then these things are not important and understanding how to manage the systems becomes less important in the hierarchy of things that a leader needs to know. It is interesting that in the academic world success is partly measured by how many times your work is cited in academic papers – the academic equivalent of a 'follow' on Twitter or a 'like' on Facebook. What's the learning equivalent and how would you manage that? As I read the work from the Organisation for Economic Co-operation and Development (OECD) on education systems I wonder when we'll see international comparisons of 'collaborativeness'. I wonder in which country the most collaboration occurs. Maybe the question is more about how communities that were once in a single physical area are now being geographically spread and, from there, understanding the communication and collaboration they create? Who heads the top-ten list for doing the most collaboration? Who heads the top-ten list for com-munication? Who heads the top-ten sharing list? These questions would best be answered by researchers and a well-researched PhD thesis perhaps.

New truth #5: me, we and us

It was a pretty ordinary Tuesday morning when my phone rang a couple of months ago. I was working on some documents and preparing for a meeting. On the phone was someone I had met at a social event; we had talked about learning and technology and many other things. She suggested I might like to talk to someone in Australia who had an exciting idea for a new venture. She thought there were synergies between what they wanted to do and the work I had done previously. In due course, I had a video call with the person in Australia and from that call a business venture was born.

The point behind the story is the way in which I was able to connect with someone over 10,000 miles away and, using technology, establish a working relationship with him and a very small team to the extent that we plotted and planned a new business venture. We shared a wide range of materials and spent a lot of time talking on video calls until we finally met face to face. Up to now the social truth has been that the only way to create economies of scale has been to physically bring people together into buildings so they can share facilities and share expertise. But that truth is now broken. We can just as easily get an expert to share using online tools as we can by getting people into physical rooms. Individ-uals can join in sessions using tools that are free at the point of delivery. Our old perceptions about economies of scale are no longer valid. I can just as easily be part of a group from my home as I can if I physically go somewhere. The new social truth is that being part of a group is no longer predicated on physical location. That changes a lot of things and has significant knock-on effects for the way we work, interact and learn. This truth has yet to permeate education systems in any meaningful way whatsoever as far as I can currently see.

So, with the cost of building and maintaining traditional learning spaces are we at a point where the economies of scale that these facilities created are breaking down? Do these physical buildings start to create cost when we can easily join in on conversations and activities from a personal mobile device using freely available Wi-Fi to facilitate the inbound connection? I believe the answers are clear. The ability to be part of a conversation from my own physical space, connected to other learners and experts who could be anywhere, makes the traditional industrial-based economies of scale break down. So, the economic arguments around having to build special buildings for learning also break down. What we need are more agile and cost-effective spaces where learners can assemble to work with their peers and experts but in new ways. The classroom or lecture theatre becomes more a space for debate and discussions; a space where you can challenge your under-standing of ideas and receive guidance on new ideas and thoughts from experts. These spaces and ways of working supplement the ability to be connected and work in groups remotely. The paradigm shifts and a new social truth emerges – to be social you don't need to be in the same physical space anymore. I explore this in a bit more detail in an article I wrote for *Computer Weekly* called 'No Classroom Required?'.[5]

In the past, the local autonomy that individuals wanted was necessarily compromised because of the requirements for economy of scale. Such is the case with testing and examinations. In a world where contempor-aneous collaboration was impossible and writing a shared document was a long and laborious process, producing collaborative documents and artefacts for assessment was very difficult, if not impossible. In the modern world, an electronic document can precisely track who contributed what, who added what and who edited what, and it can even produce clear evidence of subtle changes made by individuals. So, in the past the only way I as an individual could be assessed was by producing a unique piece of work or answering a test on my own. Any other form of testing was open to abuse as there was no objective method of seeing who had contributed what to a project. In the digital age, it is possible to audit a piece of digital work to see how the work evolved. The contribution of each individual can be objectively tracked and their input marked accordingly.

Not only does this approach allow us to mark the artefact or outcome, it allows us to understand how a group of individuals reached the necessary levels of consensus to create the artefact, including how they agreed on the shared goals and outcomes. The input of the individual – me – merges with the group, but in a way that still allows the input of the individual to be recognised. As with so much of the discussions in this book there is a considerable amount of change required – in this case, to assessment systems – to allow the opportunities offered by the digital world to be fully embraced.

So, as current assessment looks at what an individual has made of the learning process, with digital collaboration you look at each individual, combine their results and you will then get a view of the collaboration process. So, is it just a case of reinterpreting the present assessment outcomes, once for the individual and once by combining the individual scores, if this is deemed important, rather than having to totally reengineer the assessment process?

New truth #6: knowledge is no longer power

Searching for information is the lifeblood of learning. Whether it is guided research or personal research, the act of finding things out is an essential skill. Therefore, in the past those who had the keys to where to find knowledge were in a very powerful position, both personally and within society. That balance of power has fundamentally shifted. In 1998 some college geeks in the USA decided it was time to create a tool that could catalogue the information and knowledge that was being saved and shared via the Web. The Web was still relatively new but websites were proliferating, with thousands of new sites appearing each week. The rest is history, as Google was born and has gone on to currently dominate the way we search the Web. The power brokers in the 21st century are these search engines. They catalogue what is created and shared and make it available in fractions of a second.

We still have books, and publishing is not going away anytime soon. However, we can use the Web with the help of search engines to find out things instantly that might have taken days or weeks to find out before 1998. The social truth that knowledge is power is broken. The power now lies in how you use knowledge, in whether you can distinguish between fact and opinion and whether you can access the technology to carry out the search. I've shared more thoughts on why some people talk negatively about search engines and the Web in general elsewhere, so I won't repeat those ideas here. But whether we like it or not, knowledge no longer sits with the few; it sits with us all and that changes the underlying fabric of society.

New truth #7: it's all about learning

I've used the phrase 'it's all about learning' for many years. I own the URL www.allaboutlearning.org.uk and have done so since the early 2000s. The statement is a personal mantra. The sentiment this truth talks to is that learning can now be truly universal. With the growth in connectivity occurring from mobile connections and with mobile Smart devices within the reach of many more people than ever before, we are set for a democratisation of learning the like of which we have never seen. If we think that granting universal access to education in the industrial age was a revolution then what is coming is many times greater. Once we reach the political tipping points we will see learning cascading through developing countries and we will see the rise of many millions of learners who will be equipped with the latest knowledge and understanding. This will liberate populations in a way we have never seen before. With learning comes power – the power to develop and grow. At the grandest scale, we will see solutions emerging to some of the big problems we are currently working on as a species. Once the greater proportion of the human race is empowered to learn, we have the possibility to redefine the way we develop as a species.

Now this might all sound rather fanciful, but consider this: calculations that, just a few years ago, took weeks, now take seconds. This is not just because technology has advanced. We have more people working on these problems than we ever had. Ten years ago, the fastest supercomputers were made by companies like IBM, Cray and Fujitsu. Now the top spot is filled by a machine in China. We've got more of our human brains working on these developments and, therefore, we push the boundaries ever further and ever faster. Extrapolate this to the learning revolution and a new social truth emerges where everything is about learning.

New truth #8: literacy was never enough

Many have written about literacy with the clear focus in our current system evolving around the need to be able to read and write – very important skills for the present, the past and the foreseeable future. But in what context is literacy not enough? Are there circumstances where being able to read and write place us at a disadvantage, or at least not with the same advantage as others?

The idea that simply by teaching people to read and write will provide them with the necessary skills to be successful is clearly not a viable position to adopt. To be able to take a full and relevant part in society, other skills are needed. To play a meaningful part in our modern society demands much more than just literacy and numeracy. Recently, the government in England introduced computer coding into the curriculum for all learners. I believe this was done to try and address two things. Firstly, that it is good to understand how technology works, not at the mechanical level but at the intellectual level. Our digital revolution is driven by software that instructs the machines what to do. Coding can give an insight into how our digital machines work. Whilst coding is an interesting pursuit that addresses many skills, I am not totally convinced that learning to code to the level that most of our young people will achieve is going to be meaningful in the long term. Secondly, by adding coding into the curriculum it appears that we are addressing the digital revolution. But I see several contradictions here. Many organisations that teach coding then ban the very personal devices that are running the code. How does that make any sense? It seems more like paying lip service to the digital revolution.

I believe that the reality is that technology is now so part of the 'DNA' of society that to try and teach it as something separate is to create a false understanding. The essential nature of literacy is providing the necessary skills to be able to function effectively in society. Beyond reading, writing and numeracy sit a range of other skills that need to be addressed, not as discrete skills but as part of the way learning is delivered – as part of a rich and exciting approach to learning, where we use and make available to learners the best possible tools we have as a society so that they can move further and faster than we have done.

New truth #9: what happened to the family?

According to population figures and especially birth rates and mortality rates, the UK had made the transition to a post-industrial society by the early 20th century. The Demographic Transition Model (DTM), as proposed by Warren Thompson in 1929 and later developed by others, provides an accepted way of measuring and codifying the demographic changes that are indicative of this transition. The DTM defines low birth rates and low mortality rates as being indicative of a post-industrial society. A number of factors distort the figures for the UK, including migration, immigration and the effect of the First World War that saw over 700,000 British service personnel lose their lives. But the overall numbers still hold true to the model. With this shift to the post-industrial era came changes to education systems and, as the 20th century continued, changes to the nature of families.

For many years the nuclear family was considered the ideal, with a male/female couple bringing up a family together. In the pre-industrial age extended families were common, with multiple generations living in the same house or very close to each other. In the industrial age, the family unit developed and, eventually, single-generation families living in a house together became the norm (although often still living in close proximity to the extended family). As the 20th century moved on, the extended family broke down even more with each generation living in separate houses and living further apart as transport and modes of communication became more efficient. In the late 20th century things changed again. Up to the 1970s in the UK, the traditional couple family unit remained the dominant force, but as we moved through the 1970s the number of single-parent families rose, and by the 1996 census 22% of families were single-parent families. That number rose slightly to 25% by 2015, but appears to have been broadly stable for the past twenty years.

According to the Office for National Statistics, the breakdown of families in the UK in 2015 is as follows: opposite-sex married-couple families account for 59% of the total number of families; 16% of families are made up of cohabiting couples; and 25% are lone-parent families. Of the lone-parent families, 90% are female and 10% are male. Looking at the statistics in a little more depth shows that those figures have been mostly stable for the last twenty years, with a rise from 22% to 25% of lone-parent families over that period. The rise in single-parent families occurred through the 1970s when the percentage rose from 7% to 22% by the 1996 census and then to 25% by 2015.[6]

In 2015, 3.1 million children lived in single-parent families, which is 23% of all children in families; this proportion has stayed the same for over a decade. Put another way, 75% of families are still made up of two opposite-sex individuals living together, either as a married couple, in a civil partnership or cohabiting. Cohabiting partnerships are the fastest growing family type according to the most recent data. The children of these opposite-sex partnerships account for 75% of school-aged children, 25% coming from single-parent families. However, looking into the statistics still a little deeper we see that 41% of lone-parent families are in poverty compared to 24% for those from a couple family.[7] These levels of poverty are significant and create multiple issues for education systems to deal with, as well as for social services like medical services and other social support services.

I could continue to pull the statistics apart but I do not want to distil the discussion to just the numbers. I'm interested in the impact on education. For many, the new truth of a society that has a quarter of young learners from single-parent families who are more likely to be in poverty creates a new realisation of how the education system forms a stable part of people's lives. Whilst the family unit remains strong with 75% of families with children having the traditional two parents, the numbers hide the fact that many of the more deprived families are clustered around certain areas. This creates Learning Organisations where the number of needy families is far higher by percentage than the raw statistics might show. This engenders a particular need for an approach to education that understands and takes this into account. The social truth of the nuclear family being the preferred model, and the one to which we defer for the 'norms' of how people should interact, has gone completely in certain areas; but not everywhere, and not in all circumstances. This further adds weight to the argument that one system for all with one approach to testing and one way for a Learning Organisation to be structured is not going to create the most efficient way of developing a high-quality education system.

I will talk more about this in the last chapter. But one organisation that has perhaps understood this better than others is the Oasis organisation based in the UK. Founded by Steve Chalke in 1985, the organisation is built around the principle of community hubs working in areas of high deprivation, where the statistical model is significantly skewed towards families that are in need of support and that do not fit the typical and long-held model of the nuclear family. These Oasis Hubs bring together education, housing, healthcare and youth community work into a single model. If a young learner appears in a school with nowhere to live or with no food inside them then the Hub model will pull together to find solutions to these issues and not simply pass vulnerable people between agencies whilst simultaneously making them sit a test that they are going to fail because they are unable to concentrate.

New truth #10: no one trusts anyone

This might sound rather cynical and alarmist but there is definitely a trend that I've noticed where the trust we had for each other appears to be eroding. However, some organisations are developing a broader range of strategies to build trust back into interactions around learning.

In the not-too-distant past, many schools felt the need for home-school agreements where parents and students sign up to meeting the work demands that are set out by the school. High-quality relationships between Learning Organisations, learners and their guardians where appropriate have always been a hallmark of good Learning Organisations. But the need to make this more formal using agreements takes things to a new level in my view. Interestingly, some forward-looking Learning Organisations are starting to use technology to bridge the gap with students and their guardians. By using text messaging and opening up data about progress they are creating a rich and positive dialogue between home and the organisation, making the home-school agreement obsolete as they involve the wider community in the learning. Where there was little trust, they are building meaningful and purposeful dialogue around learning and achievement.

Part of the initial move towards formal agreements was to provide accountability. Where Learning Organisations were being held to account, they felt the need to formalise what they expected of their learners. If the learners did not live up to the terms of the agreement, then there was evidence to show why students were not achieving the grades they were expecting. As I write this book there is an ongoing public debate about whether parents can take children out of school for any reason other than a significant family bereavement. Parents who take children out of school for reasons that do not have the sanction of the head teacher can be fined. The debate revolves around whether children attend school regularly; currently the guidance appears to be unclear. But why is there such a focus on children missing a few days of schooling? The system should be able to cope with these absences where families are doing things together that happen to overlap with a school session.

Have we changed so much as a society that the state feels obliged to bring the law to bear on parents and students who want to spend time together? Again, as with the literacy argument, I am not condoning wholescale truancy – that is a completely separate argument. But where parents and guardians are taking children on activities that are part of the rich tapestry of life, then it looks as if the trust between parent and state has broken down to such an extent as to be very worrying.

Notes

1 Lemire, D. (2013). A Historiographical Survey of Literacy in Britain between 1780 and 1830. Available at: https://journals.library.ualberta.ca/constellations/index.php/constellations/article/viewFile/18862/14652 [2017].
2 Netmarketshare. (2017). Mobile/Tablet Top Operating System Share Trend. Available at: www.netmarketshare.com/operating-system-market-share.aspx?qprid=9&qpcustomb=1 [2017].
3 Schleicher, A. (2015). *Students, Computers and Learning: Making the Connection.* Paris: PISA, OECD Publishing.
4 Oblinger, D. & Verville, A.-L. (1999). Information Technology as a Change Agent. Available at: https://library.educause.edu/resources/1999/1/information-technology-as-a-change-agent [2017].
5 Penny, J. (2014). No Classroom Required. Available at: www.computerweekly.com/blog/ITWorks/No-classroom-required [2017].
6 Office for National Statistics. (2015). Families and Households. Available at: www.ons.gov.uk/ons/rel/family-demography/families-and-households/2015/index.html [2017].
7 Gov.UK. (2015). Households Below Average Income. Available at: www.gov.uk/government/statistics/households-below-average-income-19941995-to-20132014 [2017].

5 When does a trend become mainstream?

Technology has changed the world profoundly in a timescale that was previously unknown. In this short chapter, I want to document the key changes as they form an important backdrop to further discussions. Before we look at the technology let's just pause to think about what the speed of change means for the way our society operates. I continue to be intrigued by the following table from the UK Office for National Statistics (see Table 5.1).[1]

Look at the way the use of technology drops off with the older groups; the contrasts are quite stark. Now contemplate how the age groups reflect the typical ages of people in senior leadership positions. I appreciate that being ageist is not acceptable in the 21st century, but this is not about stopping people of a certain age from participating in something or denying access based on age. The facts are clear. Only 50% of people between 55 and 64 typically use a mobile phone to go online, whilst 89% of 16–24-year-olds use mobile devices. Move to the age range 65–74 and the percentage of those using a mobile device drops to 31. I believe there is a clear argument here that the speed of change has in effect stranded the majority of the generation who now lead our societies in a place where they are not as focused on the power of technology as are the younger generation. They are clearly intelligent people and see the changes that are happening, but the statistics would appear to show that their personal use and, therefore, their appreciation of the possibilities of this revolution are often lost on them. Maybe this is one pointer as to why we struggle to envision and create reformed education systems fit for the post-industrial age that positively embrace technology. Maybe this is why this becomes such a divisive discussion. Time and again we see education policy being created that all but ignores the role, impact and importance of technology.

Table 5.1 Use of devices to access the Internet

% of all respondents	All UK 16+	16–24	25–34	35–44	45–54	55–64	65–74	55+	65+	75+
Base	3737	519	604	602	570	578	481	1442	864	383
Ever use the Internet anywhere	87	97	97	96	93	87	72	71	58	42
% change since 2015	+1									
Broadband take-up	81	86	81	88	91	83	74	70	59	43
% change since 2015	+1									
Use mobile phone to go to online	66	89	89	84	70	50	31	33	19	6
% change since 2015	+5					+11		+8		
Use Internet at work/college	40	64	54	56	45	27	6	14	4	3
% change since 2015	0									
Use Internet at a library	7	15	8	7	4	3	4	4	3	2
% change since 2015	+1									

Tipping points

I'm always intrigued about when and how things tip over from being a trend that a few people follow to something that is mainstream and adopted by the majority of people. In Malcolm Gladwell's seminal book 'The Tipping Point', he talks about how small things can suddenly make something mainstream.[2] What is the tipping point for the shift from the industrial model to the post-industrial model? Well, in a previous chapter I looked at what the demographers define as the point at which a society moves to a post-industrial model – low birth rate and low mortality rate. So, in the UK we made that shift early in the 20th century. But what of our learning models? What are the pointers to shifts occurring that move us to a post-industrial learning model?

For technology, there have been a couple of very significant tipping points. The first was around 2010 when we got the first properly usable touch devices. Multiple developments came of age in software for mobile devices and connectivity became widespread as Wi-Fi matured and 4G appeared. With the adoption of personal mobile devices in this 'second mobile revolution', as I call it (the first was the introduction of the laptop in the mid-1990s), came the need to store data somewhere other than on physical sites, and so the widespread adoption of the 'cloud' came about. We tipped from mobility being challenging to mobility being simple and easy to adopt. The world changed. When everyone is doing something, it stops being a trend and becomes mainstream. Have you noticed how many people have devices? And with driving licences set to move to mobile platforms as well as other forms of identification, we've tipped into this post-industrial information age. But more than that we are living through what I would argue is the second phase of the digital revolution. Just as in the industrial revolution, large-scale manufacturing moved first and individuals followed; we have to date witnessed the large digitisation of back-end systems and processes in the digital revolution. From banks to retail to entertainment, our industries have embraced digital technology. The personalisation of devices is happening; just as we all adopted cars, we are all adopting personal digital devices and they are revolutionising our way of living, communicating and collaborating like never before. There are 1.7 billion individuals interacting with Facebook every month – that equates to about 66% of all those who could collaborate in this way taking an active role.

But strangely our learning models have not tipped; they're stuck in the industrial model. Well, they've not tipped at the system level anyway. On the ground, teachers and learners are making significant changes happen, whilst at the system level we are still struggling. If asked for advice the system still dictates large-scale buildings with a multitude of separate rooms that broadly accommodate thirty learners. Some people remove walls but they are still in the minority and swim against the prevailing tide. Currently I would describe our society as significantly split when it comes to learning.

The second mobile revolution

In an earlier chapter, I talked about how the first mobile revolution was born in the mid-1990s when the Web was created on the back of the Internet so that data began to flow and be shared far more widely than it had done previously. In the early 1990s the laptop computer was being developed, and although performance, battery life and weight were all poor by comparison to today, devices were developing very quickly and were selling well. However, it was not until about ten years later that tablet devices and smartphones/devices started to be viable.

From about 2007 onwards we saw what I call the 'second mobile revolution' taking off in a pervasive manner. Personal mobile devices exploded onto the marketplace very quickly. The Android and iOS operating systems drove things forward, as did Symbian and Blackberry. Eventually Symbian declined as Android increased market share. The Blackberry OS had significant growth and popularity but then decreased significantly. By 2016 there was a rich ecosystem of devices and operating systems, as illustrated in Table 5.2.

As I've noted elsewhere, change happens very fast and without doubt the table will be out of date almost as soon as this book is published. It will be fascinating to look back in five years and measure how much change has taken place.

We tipped

We've reached a tipping point in technology. We have mature devices with intuitive touch-based interfaces. There are multiple versions of devices in a variety of sizes and configurations. There are devices that can make and receive phone calls and devices that have that

Table 5.2 Operating systems and devices

	Devices				
OS	Watch	Smartphone	Tablet	'Laptop'	'Desktop'
⌠Chrome	No	No	No	Chromebook	Chromebook
⌡Android (Wear)	Yes	Yes	Yes	No	No
⌠iOS/Watch OS	Yes	iPhone/iPod/iPad		No	No
⌡OSX	No	No	No	MacBook	iMac/Mac Mini
Windows 10	Band	Yes	Yes	Yes	Yes

functionality missing but equally provide a wide range of other functions. Technology will develop and in five years' time I will need to update this section with new devices and interfaces. But I do not believe that we will see the diminution of the tipping point that occurred between 2007 and 2010. I believe that history will record those years as a defining point for what is was to be a digitally mobile citizen. The Enabling Technologies I outlined in the Foreword were there to support this significant change and from this has flowed a significant shift in our society that is changing the way we interact and collaborate.

Technology was no longer some trendy thing that a few people tinkered with, it became mainstream. It supported the delivery of critical services and as we move away from 2010 we are seeing that services are not being made optionally available via technology but that technology is being used as the preferred way to access services. From voting to collecting state benefits, we've tipped, and the option to not use digital systems is fast disappearing. Yet if you look at our education system and at how we prepare our learners for this online approach, we see no support, guidance or advice on how we should teach the necessary skills.

I have referenced elsewhere the points at which technological developments have supported very rapid change and then the adoption of technology. I have talked about two mobile revolutions. The first was triggered by the early promise of the Internet and the subsequent development of the Web that spawned the growth in mobile laptop devices. This happened in the mid-1990s. The second mobile revolution happened a decade later between 2007 and 2010. The rise of the touch interface, the increased power of mobile processors and the ability to better manage power consumption saw the proliferation of personal mobile devices. The tipping points here were technological developments that then allowed the mass adoption of new social and working practices. I am often involved in discussions around whether we chase the technology too much, but I always see it the other way around. I believe that technology has a long way to go to catch up with what we require it to do for us. We can still write science fiction that paints pictures of how technology can support our lives in ways that we can only dream of achieving. People lead the way and technology struggles to keep up. Take the touch interface. We've been using our fingers to point, touch and find out about things since . . . forever. It was in that second mobile revolution that we got the tools that allowed us to use that natural way of interacting with the world. We have a long way to go and many tipping points to encounter before technology will support us in doing things more efficiently and effectively than we do at the moment. As with all change, we will look back in ten years with affection at the devices we were using, wondering how we managed to be productive.

Notes

1 Office for National Statistics. (2016). Internet Access – Households and Individuals: 2015. Available at: www.ons.gov.uk/peoplepopulationandcommunity/householdcharacteristics/homeinternetandsocialmediausage/bulletins/internetaccesshouseholdsandindividuals/2015-08-06 [2017].
2 Gladwell, M. (2000). *The Tipping Point*. London: Little, Brown Book Group.

6 Online by default

There was a time that when people wrote articles and other texts they were either written in longhand or typed using a manual typewriter. The vast majority of written material is now created on a digital device. Even those authors who still prefer to write in longhand – and there are still a significant number – will have their manuscripts typed into a digital medium to support the editing and revision process. Quite simply, the world has gone digital whether you like it or not; everything we read that is printed is at least edited, if not created, on digital devices. The moveable typesetting process that revolutionised the printing process all those years ago has been replaced by computers that link automatically to the printing machine at the press of a button. On-demand printing is with us and will slowly take over the world of publishing as we move deeper into the 21st century. Our 'Third Millennium Learners', as I call them, are adept at using devices for the creation and manipulation of a wide range of digital artefacts. And these digital artefacts are then shared using the Web and the wide range of tools that now exist to share a wide variety of content.

The UK government talks of the NHS becoming digital by default and paperless by 2020 or 2022 – the goalposts have moved. The ability to share everything using the Web and the underlying connectivity of the Internet has made it possible to think of everything being online by default. For many organisations, there is no conscious decision whether to publish something online or not, it is there by default. Networks that were once confined to physical buildings are now interconnected and can publish at the push of a button. Everything that is created electronically has the potential to be instantly shared with one or several billion people.

The point is that there is no longer a conscious decision needed as to whether content should be made available online or not – it is simply online by default. This is in stark contrast to previous ages.

Pre-industrial societies relied on handwritten documents and books were often scarce and expensive to produce and to procure. Thankfully printing was invented or we would have lost so much wisdom, entertainment and knowledge. Without the first folio of Shakespeare's plays we would have lost much of the literature we love, and that has influenced the very fabric of our language as well as much else in our society.

I am fascinated by the rapid transformation that is taking place in the media industry. At the start of the digital revolution very little content was available that was not broadcast. The 'one-to-many' model of broadcast television was taken for granted, as the way that entertainment was going to be delivered by television. Videotapes offered a way of recording and watching at your leisure but the linear nature of the tape made the ability to jump between programmes or sections of programmes very difficult. If anyone reading this book used videotapes in their teaching as I did you will remember the process of getting a tape to the right place each time you wanted to show a particular piece of video to a class. DVDs changed things a little but the players were always relatively expensive and recording to DVDs never really took off in the way that recording onto videotape had done. Anyway, by the time DVDs came along the online revolution was already starting to take hold. Because, like publishing, all television content was being stored digitally, the move from storing it to putting it online was a very short and easy step for broadcasters to take. In a very few years it became possible to put anything online and make it accessible from a computer or Smart TV using the facilities provided by the Internet and the Web. Programmes began to be cut up into smaller pieces and posted online, giving access to specific ideas, news items and supporting a new approach for viewers. Digital content became downloadable and was available when not connected to the Internet. Viewing habits changed and, as I write this book in 2017, they are probably undergoing the biggest shift since the birth of broadcasting. More and more people are accessing content using an on-demand model, watching what they want when they want it. Sometimes we still digitally record our content but more and more we are simply streaming our favourite content when it is convenient. Broadband speeds have increased and so has the technology to compress video streams so they use less bandwidth. Taken together, these two development processes make streaming content viable for a large number of people.

The BBC, funded by a licence fee, has one of the most comprehensive portfolios of digital content anywhere in the world. Up until this year

(2017) you could access all of that content without paying the licence fee. It has just been announced that this will change so that viewing via the BBC iPlayer will require the viewer to have some kind of licence; exactly how that will be enforced is not yet clear. The position with digital publishing and digital video has developed very fast and continues to develop as new ideas and technologies are deployed. In the same way, music delivery has transformed dramatically over the past five years. Music became digital before video. The amounts of data required for an audio track are substantially less than for a piece of video and so the industry was forced to transform faster, to the point where the number of times a song is downloaded now counts towards the position of the song in the charts. In fact, more and more music is now being released in purely digital streaming formats. Physical sales of CDs continue to fall as the transition to digital music is almost complete. The industry is still struggling with payment models and how to monetise every digital opportunity, but these too are developing rapidly. I believe that payment models for digital music need to take a radical shift – away from paying for the music and towards taking a cut of the bandwidth charges users pay to access the content. This would create more disintermediation and reshape the business models, but, in my view, it has to happen; just selling the music in a world where digital copying makes sharing very easy is not a long-term business model. In the future, we will see a growing move to the mobile network providers combining music and video as part of the cost for connectivity. This has already started.

Linear versus 'manipulable' – the untapped paradigm shift

So, what of learning? Has this revolution in audio and video content becoming digital had as profound an effect in education as it has in other areas? This is not a simple question to answer. The digital nature of content and content delivery has profoundly affected the way people access knowledge and has profoundly affected the way people learn. Has this permeated to our education systems? Not to the degree that it should have. The digital revolution has brought about three massive changes to the way we can all access and use information. The world has become *digital*, *mobile* and *personal*, whilst education has remained steadfastly *analogue*, *static* and *generalist*. This revolution of the post-industrial era has and is passing education organisations by at an alarming rate. The challenge that the education system appears to be unable or unwilling to shake off is the industrial model of one teacher teaching thirty same-age peers. As long as that model persists then anything that is personalised becomes impossible to manage unless you change some of the fundamental building blocks. But this is not about tinkering at the edges, there are some significant changes needed. As Andreas Schleicher of the OECD says, simply adding 21st-century technologies to 20th-century pedagogies actually makes things worse, not better.[1]

Below I have listed some of the common reasons we are told digital resources and approaches are not successfully adopted in education systems:

1. The lack of support and advice to help educators tap the potential of the 'manipulable', non-linear nature of digital content.

   Actually, teachers are not the issue, it's the organisations they have to work within that cause the problems.

2. The advice on how to build IT networks in Learning Organisations. The advice is twenty years old and has not been updated.

   For some reason, the local area network persists in education. The notion of being part of a distributed cloud-based network strikes fear into the heart of the education establishment. This is mainly through ignorance rather than any rationale reasoning.

3. The wholescale production of learning materials in digital format appears to create great controversy.

   Mostly people are still taking a paper-based document and placing it in a digital repository as a portable document format (PDF) or some other sharable format. That is not embracing the digital age . . . well, in one way it could be argued that it does, but that approach does not take advantage of the array of opportunities going digital offers.

4. Access to devices in Learning Organisations gets mired in all kinds of challenges, from moral arguments, to financial arguments, to technology companies pushing certain devices as being the only tenable solution.

   If most learners have a device then what's the issue here? Well, there are many that are well rehearsed and used as barriers.

5   The types of devices that are purchased and their suitability for the use to which they are being put.

Education still buys desktops, followed by laptops and then some tablet devices. This misses the possibilities of personal digital devices completely.

Each of the reasons above, on their own, creates a block to realising the potential that the digital revolution can bring about in learning, but combine two or three of them and the whole thing falls apart and the potential and benefit is lost. I'll explore each in a little more detail below.

1) Manipulable content

In the late 1990s I was involved in some interesting conversations on the nature of digital content. As the digital era took off it was clear that content was no longer linear. It was possible and easy to break what had been, up to this point, linear pieces of content into smaller pieces that could be accessed in a simple way using easy-to-operate tools. By 2005 YouTube was born and has been used ever since. Its usage has grown and it shows no signs of waning in popularity. In effect, YouTube provides a way of sharing pieces of digital content that are accessible using simple search criteria. This content can be short ten-second pieces to hour-long traditional programmes. YouTube provides a simple way of sharing video content that people are making in their own time. Many of the teachers who are leading the revolution I reference in the Foreword to this book are regularly creating and uploading high-quality digital content for their students. Much of this is not officially sanctioned and is often in addition to the traditional textbooks and other traditional ways of delivering content. The rationale for not embedding the YouTube approach into more teaching is often lost in the issues that surround how Learning Organisations build their networks (see the following section 'Building networks'). Also, there is still, as I mention elsewhere, something that makes textbooks with their high-quality production values appear superior to digital content. Good textbooks go through a rigorous set of editing and checking before publication. It is a well-understood and well-rehearsed process that guarantees the quality of the finished product. There are not, as yet, the same processes around digital content. The investment required to get to that level of rigour is substantial and the commercial market for the end product is still limited by the issues around the way networks are being built in Learning Organisations. There is, however, one example that I have seen that ticks all the boxes around production values, the checking of content and paying the same attention to detail as we see in the production of our much-loved analogue textbooks. The organisation was originally called Espresso, and is now Discovery Education in recognition of the purchase of Espresso by Discovery Education in 2013. The original company was launched in 1997. One of its co-founders brought to the company a unique set of skills. The person in question was Lewis Bronze. He had been the editor of the BBC's flagship children's programme *Blue Peter* for eight years and had overseen the continued success of the programme. His understanding of how to create high-quality digital content for a young audience was unsurpassed and the production values that underpinned all BBC production were the best in the world. Lewis took those skill sets and went about creating the best-quality digital content for education that has ever been made. I bought into the content way back at the start of the venture in 1997 for a school I was working in at the time. The Internet was in its infancy and the bandwidth required to access and download the content was very expensive. To overcome this the company supplied a satellite dish so that the content could be updated weekly. Today the content is delivered over broadband, but to be involved at the start and see how the technical hurdles were overcome was inspiring.

So, it is possible to create high-quality digital content for learning that has high production values, is accurate and is made available to a wide audience. The business model that would see an explosion in this kind of high-quality content is, however, hampered by poor-quality network designs that are still being rolled out in our education systems.

2) Building networks

So, building a network in a Learning Organisation has nothing to do with the educators; is it purely a matter for the technology people? Not so. Educators need to specify and make clear what they need their infrastructure to enable. This has to include access to digital content in all its forms, as well as a design that is flexible and can be easily and cost-effectively developed as technology develops. Some Learning Organisations I visit – I was going to say all but that would be an overstatement – have networks that were implemented ten years ago and many use designs that have changed very little in twenty years. In the interim, the skills needed to keep the design up to date have been neglected and the design has been frozen in time. Furthermore, if you look for reference designs for education networks they are non-existent. This whole area is an afterthought and not at the centre of the strategy. The reason this is the case resides with the lack of triangulation between highly effective schools and technology. The two are consistently kept separate. The rationale for this separation is weakly presented or not presented at all.

In the following chapters, I discuss various research from a number of sources into what makes effective schools. I look at how technology can be applied to these characteristics to enhance the effectiveness of the organisation. In those sections and again here we are, however, looking at what happens when we add our post-industrial tools to an existing system, and that is dangerous. As Andreas Schleicher puts it, 'adding 21st-century technologies to 20th-century teaching practices will just dilute the effectiveness of teaching'.[2]

This is happening all the time and it's slowing reform and creating a false view of how our systems need to reform. I will tackle this further in Chapter 9, whilst here I would urge those looking at reforming the system to be wary of this approach of imposing our 21st-century tools onto 20th-century practices. In fact, many of the practices actually comprise 19th-century approaches to learning, making the dilution even more damaging.

Third Millennium Learning Networks

For a number of years, I have been talking about building Third Millennium Learning Networks. The phrase was created to drive discussion. It hides within it a question that is a challenge to define what has changed in network design and then challenges those tasked with building systems to think more broadly about how they should design their systems for Learning Organisations in the future.

The world of networks has changed dramatically over the last ten years, but if you look at many Learning Organisations you would think that nothing has changed. Physical buildings have dictated the model for how networks are built and because Learning Organisations are still predominantly in fixed locations then the motives to develop the design of networks is low. This leads to designs being implemented that are twenty years old. They assume the traditional client–server model where the core of the network sits on the physical site. Whilst there is nothing wrong with this design approach it does create considerable challenges when you want to extend the learning to other physical sites or want students to continue their learning away from the physical site.

The client–server model tends to emphasise the client-device-image model where a large software image is developed and deployed to a traditional desktop or laptop. Mobile device management is seen as an add-on to the environment, with mobile devices often seen as challenging to manage. This perceived challenge of managing devices then provokes various reactions in the way mobile devices, and especially personal mobile devices, are treated and managed. Many organisations move to Bring Your Own Device (BYOD) strategies that are often not bring your own at all – frequently the organisation sets up a scheme for learners to buy certain devices that they know can be managed. Learners end up with two devices: their own device and one the organisation has dictated. This costs parents and guardians extra money. In the modern world forget BYOD – we need to support 'Using My Own Device' (UMOD). We need networks and systems that are flexible enough to provide a high-quality experience to learners using a range of devices.

An interesting view can be seen if you look at what happened to multi-academy trusts in England as they grew and how, under the Building Schools for the Future (BSF) investment programme, many acquired new multi-million-pound buildings. Some grew to eighty schools with multiple new buildings and the refurbishment of existing buildings. Thirty or forty schools in a group is not uncommon. All the new-build and refurbishment projects had an allocation for ICT. However, very few of these trusts took a holistic view of the opportunity they were being given. To be fair, there was no guidance around that suggested doing anything else; in fact, most guidance was to treat each project as a separate entity. Therefore, they looked at each project separately and created multiple unconnected networks, duplicating systems in school after school. Each system needs an expensive on-site team to manage it and skills, systems and costs are duplicated. The opportunity to rationalise systems and share systems to avoid duplication and reduce costs was taken by very few of these organisations. Somehow, the Multi-Academy Trust providing such guidance and support was cast as interference by some. Still now some argue that supporting this model where cost is duplicated is fine and that to do anything else would be seen as being heavy-handed. It makes no sense for any organisation to duplicate costs needlessly. With the massive strides in the remote management of IT systems the potential for cost savings are significant. Also, as systems start to age, these groups are faced with massive bills for the renewal of solutions that are over-specified and built around these twenty-year-old designs. A design does not have the Internet or the Web at its core; it has the client–server model and more than often a New Technology File System (NTFS) – a system that does not allow easy communication with TCP/IP protocols and systems that have been implemented in a way that locks content onto the site. Wireless provision is an afterthought and often poorly implemented.

There is a move to using systems like Office 365 and Google Apps (G Suite). These have started being used for email and for basic sharing and collaborating on documents. However, integrating these tools into legacy systems in a meaningful way is very challenging. In short, many of the reasons for the slow adoption of post-industrial working practices in education can be centred around lack of support and advice that Learning Organisations are getting on how to build, maintain and develop their networks.

In summary then, the design for a modern learning network is not client–server – it's a Web-based personal connection model that sup-ports all device types, irrespective of who owns them. The designs must have wireless as the core component of the design. Wired connections for devices are for legacy support only and are not the future. Think of wireless differently. Think about working with mobile providers. They could install a 4G solution that directly hooks into a private cloud environment. Any network in the 21st century does not stop at the physical edges of the building; it extends beyond the physical walls and into the Internet and the Web. Your network, therefore, has to secure and connect in new ways that serve the learning, rather than making man-aging the environment easy for the technical team.

This painful change process is not new. We have experienced such things before. I was reading a book on the history of railways by Simon Bradley entitled *The Railways: Nation, Network and People*.[3] I would highly recommend reading it even though it runs to 550 pages. As I read this well-crafted book I was struck by how the changes he was describing around railways and transport were being described in ways that reflected the discussions we hear today about technology. As interesting as the book itself is the short story about how I came across the book. I was on a train travelling to London and across the aisle from me a lady was reading the book and periodically reading sections aloud to her partner. Being fascinated by what she was reading I asked for the title of the book. We had a brief conversation. As we drew into London the lady asked if I would like the ISBN and title of the book. I was able to tell her that I had already found, bought and downloaded the book onto my smartphone and was reading away. A hard copy followed shortly in the post to my home address, but the immediacy of the experience on the train and being able to start reading straight away was an interesting pointer to the way things have changed.

3) Digital learning materials

The wholescale production of learning materials into digital formats appears to create great controversy. There are still two deeply divided schools of thought. One view is well represented by the comments made by Andreas Schleicher of the OECD. I've already quoted the Foreword to the OECD book, *Students, Computers and Learning*, but I'd like to use one more quote to focus a discussion. Schleicher references digital texts by saying:

> Why should students be limited to a textbook that was printed two years ago, any maybe designed ten years ago, when they could have access to the world's best and most up-to-date textbook? Equally important, technology allows teachers and students to access specialised materials well beyond textbooks, in multiple formats, with little time and space constraints.[4]

digital Resources

However, a counter view is that textbooks are a legitimate resource and should continue to be used. Well-written textbooks will be factually correct and a definitive source. After all, the facts about the First World War, for example, will remain constant. Also, a textbook written by a respected author and published by a respected publishing house will be checked and often peer reviewed to ensure that the facts are correct. Such text will also be clearly identifiable as presenting opinion. Some might also argue that there is a certain irony that some schools have devices sitting in the cupboard gathering dust as they age and cease to function due to software upgrades.

The two views can both be seen to have valid points, but certain things do change. Take population numbers or economic data and a different story emerges. A textbook can very well set out the underlying economic models but will fail to provide up-to-date economic data. As in all things the options with digital content versus analogue content is not a binary decision. Each have their uses and each have their strengths and associated weaknesses.

All too often the effectiveness of digital content is hampered by the devices being used to access the content. Technology collecting dust is something that many schools experience. Too many devices are purchased out of a whim or from a feeling that organisations must keep up with each other. Very few decisions are made in a hard-headed way based on a factual analysis of need. I'll cover this more in point 5) below. For now though, I'd like to end this point by saying the following: digital learning materials can be exceptional. They can explain ideas and concepts in ways that will never be possible using paper diagrams. Three-dimensional fly-throughs of the human body explain how systems work in a way that no amount of paper-based diagrams will ever be able to deliver. That is clear and unarguable. How we access these materials and the devices we choose for access are critical to making the use of digital learning materials successful.

4) Access to devices

I'd like to really break some models that are so ingrained in the rules of technology in learning that to even talk about doing things differently makes many people rise up with a cadre of excuses. Few of the reasons are valid, most are raised because the status quo is being challenged. Just as the client–server model is dead so is the notion of all devices being owned by the organisation. In the client–server model, the institutional ownership of devices made sense. To get the machines to access resources on the network, an image was needed, and that image had to be created by the on-site technical team. But mobility, Smart devices and cloud-based solutions broke that model . . . only many people in Learning Organisations have not worked this out yet. I recently saw a presentation at a higher education conference and the message from a global thought-leader at Gartner was that your network no longer stops at your physical boundaries, so think differently. We often hear people describing technology as disruptive, meaning that it is impossible to continue to operate in the same way as you have done in the past. The list of Enabling Technologies I outlined at the start of the book are not just enabling, they are disruptive. They are forcing new ways of working within many organisations.

As the second mobile revolution takes hold, the Learning Organisations that take a lead will build their IT systems differently. If they are really smart they won't need on-site servers, they won't need to manage complex server-based user profiles and they won't need to spend hours each day checking backups and checking if storage systems are slowing down because they are filling up so fast due to digital content. In fact, I predict that networks in their current form will wither and disappear. With collaborative systems becoming easily and cheaply available from robust cloud systems, the complex management activities will disappear. Users will use their own devices and they will blur the boundaries between learning and personal data.

The killer argument that is presented by educators working with learners up to the age of sixteen is that some families are not able to fund a device for their children and, indeed, some do not want to fund a device. There are clearly cases where poverty means a device is not attainable but there are models that will allow provision to be made. Access to devices is not a problem. Helping senior leaders understand how to make schemes viable and effective is at the heart of the challenge. As with many things this is a social issue and not a technical issue.

5) Devices – fit for purpose

The number and types of devices are exploding. In a little over seven years, from 2010 to 2017, we have gone from a relatively small number of device form factors to multiple devices and form factors. As an example, my wife's Facebook memories just popped up the following exchange between her and a friend from 2010. My wife wrote on her page:

> *Very excited, James got lent a pre launch ipad to try and it's brilliant!!!!! Everyone needs, one, start saving!!!*

Friend replies:

> *Just one Q . . . what's an ipad?*

My wife replied:

> *Go and google it now girl!!!! It's a sort of oversized iPhone, totally amazing, very intuitive, kids just sat down and started using it without any help, gotta get one!*

Now, six years on as I write this book in 2017, I doubt there's anyone who's not heard of the iPad, so ubiquitous has it become. The touch interface revolutionised the way we work with computers, as I've described elsewhere. Since 2010 we've seen multiple-sized touch devices from multiple vendors, some with a physical keyboard and some without, some with 'pens' as well as ever thinner and lighter laptops and ever smaller desktop devices. Some devices were just aimed at reading digital books whilst others are multipurpose devices.

We looked at the diversity of devices and operating systems in Chapter 5 and, as the Table 5.1 shows, the range of devices and associated operating systems available have made consumer choices considerably more complex than when the only real alternative was a Microsoft Windows environment on desktops or laptops.

But the enthusiasm for new devices and the growing choice of device types hides some important things that need to be considered – are they fit for purpose and being used to the best effect?

Certain devices are good at certain things and trying to get them to perform certain functions creates a poor user experience. So, when thinking about devices, it is really important to focus on what you want to do with the device. What follows is not new and has been discussed by many before so I'll share in as short a way as possible what others have already documented. I will, however, briefly explore the idea of 21st-century pedagogies, or at least how 20th-century pedagogies can develop and be made more powerful.

When you learn, you do basically four things: you *consume* pre-prepared content by reading, listening or watching, you *create* work to show your understanding, you *share* what you have created and, as you do these, you *collaborate* with others. N.B.

I briefly summarise these activities and how they develop with 21st-century tools in Table 6.1. There are challenges. I know from my own personal experience that working collaboratively on a document when several people are adding text at the same time is a very different and new experience; it needs practice and it needs to be used at appropriate times.

Here's the challenge for everyone wanting to using technology to support more powerful pedagogy: the devices that do one thing well, like consuming content, often don't do other things well, like creating content. We all know this to be true. After all, someone invented the printing press because producing handwritten books was time-consuming and expensive. Try typing a 2000-word essay on a smartphone and

Table 6.1 Modes of access to information

Activity	20th century	21st century	Enabling Technology
Consume	Read books, talk to teachers/lecturers, watch some video and listen to some audio	Read, access digital content, access remote texts, access other expertise remotely	Web, Internet, digital content, connected networks, personal devices
Create	Write longhand text, draw/illustrate	Write longhand, digital text, digital images, create and manipulate various digital artefacts	Text and word processors, simple-to-use apps on mobile devices
Share	Hand work in, hand in exercise book	Email, SMS, collaborative folders, joint document creation	Email, SMS, Web tools, social media
Collaborate	Talk to teachers/lecturers, talk with same-age peers	Video, audio tools, shared digital spaces, collaborative document creation and editing	Email, SMS, Web tools, social media

you'll soon get the point that it's a brilliant device for finding and reading things but not so brilliant at creating. So, any device strategy has to be carefully thought out. It comes back to the curriculum in many ways. A deep understanding of what you are asking learners to do at certain points in the curriculum is needed so that a device strategy can be created that covers all eventualities. This can be tough as it often means working across platforms and operating systems. It ultimately requires a degree of flexibility and agility from everyone involved. This flexibility still requires time to be fully embedded in developing the skills of both learners and teachers/lecturers alike. Support and training can take us so far, but attitude and the will to succeed is needed to make the last mile.

From text to email to apps

Short Message Service (SMS) was a function of the mobile phone revolution that, in my view, sparked in users the realisation that mobile devices could change the way we interact with each other. Whilst email and mobile phone calls were in themselves major milestones, they were in effect an updating of previous ways of communicating. We've been writing letters to each other for centuries and all email did was make the delivery process faster and cheaper than using the paper equivalent. The quantity of email any one of us can create far exceeds the volume of handwritten letters that we can write. So, email was revolutionary in its own way, but it was not a new way of communicating – we even called it e...mail, so close was the fit to the previous model. The delivery method was revolutionary, not the mode of communication. SMS messaging was a new paradigm. The initial character limit and the instant response provided for a new shorthand way of communicating much more akin to the brief interactions professionals have when using radio communications – essential facts only and keep it as short as possible. I'll come back to this mode of communication in a short while as it bears a massive similarity to Twitter.

This shift from mail to email did, however, have far more profound consequences for the way we run our lives and for the way we run our society. When we sent a handwritten letter to an organisation we knew it could take several days to be delivered to the intended recipient and then it had to be read and a reply had to be written. All this took time and allowed organisations to operate at a certain pace where the time to communicate was an accepted part of the wider equation. With email, all that changed. Firstly, everyone got their own personal mail address with their own personal inbox. No longer could an organisation hide behind an anonymous postal address. If, as some still do, they use the dreadful 'info@whatevercompany.com' then they tend to put themselves at a competitive disadvantage when their competitors are giving a named email address like james@thisismycompany.com and where James responds quickly and efficiently to the email. The speed at which we can now exchange thoughts and detailed ideas has accelerated – although I'm not sure how much of that has filtered down to our public servants. Each time I try and communicate with someone in officialdom I frequently get a response that tells me how busy they are and it will take a week for them to reply to my email. The method of delivery may have changed but the time frame for response is still very much of the 20th or even 19th century. Mobile phones made the phone a more convenient tool for obvious reasons. Untethering the device from a fixed point made it possible to recast the way we communicate in a way that mimicked the communication we have been involved in for thousands of years. But, again, here we often see organisations hiding behind monolithic phone filtering systems. Call centres have replaced phones on desks but mobile numbers are often hidden.

Do we have here one of the reasons why the education systems are so out of step with much of what is going on in our current society? In our pre-industrial and industrial ages everyone understood that a letter took time to be delivered and responded to. In 1805, it took 37 hours for the news of the victory over the combined French and Spanish forces at the battle of Trafalgar to reach London from Falmouth. With the news of victory came the news of the death of Nelson. Such information would circumnavigate the globe in seconds today. Sometimes I feel that governments lament the long communication time frames of the past. Making considered decisions takes time, but in a world that expects everything instantly, challenges emerge.

One of the most interesting aspects in learning is the use of social media. There are those who would brief against its use, and it can indeed be distracting when it becomes an obsession. But take a look at what teachers are doing on Twitter. They are sharing ideas, instantly sharing what works, sharing how things can be developed and sharing when new approaches to traditional topics are yielding real benefits in the classroom. Ideas spread instantly across the planet, not just in the physical building. Some of these ideas stick and change the way learning is delivered. The power of this medium has yet to be tapped fully. Most of the use by teachers is what I describe as 'under the radar' – it is not an officially sanctioned approach but a way that has evolved. Really great teachers are using these instant tools to generate a wealth of new ideas and approaches. There are some solutions that look to mimic social media within the closed environment of a school with some inclusion of parents. Somehow these officially sanctioned solutions lack something that is offered by the global communities of Twitter and the like. I would suggest that the whole attraction is to share beyond your community and get new ideas that nourish the teachers. Limiting to your immediate community does not offer that allure of being able to share to a global audience.

So, we live in a circular world; or at least a world where we are in an upward spiral – where approaches are revisited and refined. What started off with SMS messaging and email developed into other ways of sharing, like Twitter, Snapchat, Facebook and other platforms, where quick and short exchanges point people to various locations where in-depth analyses of new ideas are taking place. This contemporary approach to sharing sits well with the research around what makes great Learning Organisations. The observations from many experts show that training teachers and lecturers in formal settings is sub-optimal, but getting people together to share ideas in a professional setting really does make a difference. Getting teachers together is expensive and has to happen during times when they are meant to be working with the learners. So, using the facilities of social media to share ideas creates a dynamic and real-time interaction between staff. Many of the interactions that start on social media develop into Teachmeets – events where teachers spontaneously get together to share ideas and teaching resources. Again, these events happen beneath the radar of official professional development activities, but are redefining the face of how teachers and lecturers share high-quality ideas in this post-industrial age.

Breadth

Many years ago, when I was an aspiring senior leader in a large school, I was sent on a course called Celebrating Success. The idea of the course was to share ways in which Learning Organisations could showcase the high-quality work that students are doing and use this showcase as a way of creating an environment where hard work and success could be celebrated. This course was held in the mid-1990s, well before the advent of cost-effective and ubiquitous devices were available. The methods we had for sharing success were quite limited, being mostly to do with using traditional photographs, displays of student work and showcase events. When I look at my social media timelines today I see a wide range of educators instantly sharing events, celebrating the achievements of learners across the globe at the touch of a screen. This powerful approach to sharing success has a very high motivating factor for organisations. When images or ideas are picked up and shared across multiple organisations and by tens of thousands or even tens of millions of people then we know we have defined and are accessing a new audience that would previously never have been privy to these local successes. I've developed one aspect of this in a later chapter where I look at how our 21st-century tools can allow us to have access to a local, national and global audience in a way that was previously impossible. People and organisations attract thousands and even millions of followers that take an interest in and share the activities that learners are taking part in each day. In this way, learners become not just consumers of knowledge but creators of important artefacts and insights that are then used by others to redefine the way our world sees and defines certain things. Much is made of 'trolling' when social media is discussed, as is cyberbullying. Both these activities are worrying and need careful consideration. But to ignore the place of social media in the lives of learners is not the way forward. If Learning Organisations and the education they seek to provide is meant to prepare people for life then these tools need to be embraced and positively used, not ignored. Our learners have these devices and the Office for National Statistics data tell us that 75% of young people have social media profiles. Banning the use of devices and social media in the classroom will not stop these tools and software being used outside the learning day. Just as education did with drugs education and sex education, learners need to be helped to make sensible and measured decisions. A cry for abstinence or a call for banning devices will not support our learners to make the right decisions.

The ability to use these tools to share ideas in concise formats has developed and continues to develop. From a starting point with humble SMS messages we now have video-sharing sites, Twitter for text, images and video, we have Snapchat for various quick ways of sharing ideas and content, we have Pinterest for sharing images and collections of images around specific topics, we have Facebook for sharing ideas, video, audio and for online chat, we have Skype, we have Facetime and by the time you read this we'll have more. All of them speak to the core and fundamental message of the 21st century: life is complex, by breaking ideas into small chunks, sharing with colleagues and experts we can move forward on several fronts at once and therefore support a rich diversity and development of ideas.

Although we've looked at the way our tools have developed from SMS to Twitter and other social media along the way, we should acknowledge that these tools are still in their infancy. We've been writing for centuries, millennia even, and printing books for hundreds of years. We've been using these digital tools for tens of years at most and in some cases a handful of years. I do become exasperated at those who simply dismiss these rich and exciting tools for learning without understanding the context and possibilities that they open up. It will take more years for these tools to embed themselves but we must be open about the possibilities and not dismiss them and try to measure the impact they have in terms of simple cause-and-effect economics. The effects will be long-term and will create new paradigms for working together. Just as writing and printing have developed a well understood and used paradigm, so will these new tools, and in time they will be as well used and understood. Until then, however, we must not dismiss these tools. We must embrace their use and develop new understandings to benefit our learners. Maybe we need a new age of leaders to emerge before these tools are effectively embedded. As the current crop of leading-edge exponents of these new tools move up through the leadership ranks they will bring about the revolution that is required. I do hope so as the current impasse is neither sustainable nor acceptable in a century that is seeing the digital revolution continue at an ever-faster pace. Just as the industrial revolution brought about change, so is the current digital revolution, and we should embrace it for education and learning.

So how does all this reflect back on education leadership?

Education organisations are one of the last bastions of the industrial leadership model; you can't get to the top unless you have served your apprenticeship and then worked your way up through a Learning Organisation, learning the ways things are done. Two critical issues emerge from this model: serving your apprenticeship takes time and as you serve your time you work with others who are considered masters at what they do. Inevitably, however, the masters of their craft have got to their current position through the diligent use of approaches and practices that are, by their very nature, dated. Let me explain this in a bit more detail. If you take an apprenticeship to become a master carpenter then the majority of tools and ways of jointing and preparing wood have changed very little in hundreds of years. Some tools have become mechanised to speed up the processes of cutting and finishing, but the joints and approaches to making items has not changed. Therefore, the apprentice that learns how to construct the perfect mortise and tenon joint is as relevant today as they were 100 years ago. There simply are no better ways of securely joining wood for the uses that the mortise and tenon joint fulfils. With our Learning Organisations, our approach to leadership tends to reinforce approaches to learning, many of which are outdated or look backwards for inspiration rather than looking sideways and forwards. Many traditional approaches to education do work to deliver a certain kind of learning. But is it the kind of learning that our society needs in the 21st century? Looking at the responses from employers, one can strongly argue that it is not.

The debate gets rather complicated as positions are defended on the grounds of tradition and arguments about how standards were better in the past. But as we explored previously, things have substantially changed and are still changing. If we look to the past and the pre-industrial and industrial eras, literacy and numeracy were the preserve of the few, not the masses. Education was the preserve of the few, not the masses, and approaches to learning and teaching were far behind what we know and understand today. So, what do we mean when we talk of traditional standards and traditional values? I have to say that when I look at these arguments in detail there is little more than a mythical impressionist view of a landscape that appeared to show much promise, but when a clear light is shone on it the landscape that is revealed is not the promised land that we thought it was.

One thing is clear about education and leadership – having a knowledge of how the education system operates is important. Managing and leading education organisations requires an understanding of the complex arrangements that government has put in place. It also requires an understanding of how to manage the day-to-day operations of an ever-changing organisation. But these are very much the operational aspects of education leadership. The real leadership requirements sit at a higher level. In industry, those tipped for top leadership positions take an MBA course. This allows them to look at how organisations work and to gain ideas and experience on how to lead effectively. In England, we have tried many times to support education leaders in order to gain experience, but all of the models have been what I call 'closed systems'; that is, the courses have been run specifically for and by educators and have been aimed at leading Learning Organisations with content and examples that rarely look more widely at how other organisations work.

What is this utopian past that we look back to? Firstly, I think we need to be clear that there is also a peculiar viewpoint that the English nation has on all this. The education system in England is multi-faceted, as previously pointed out. Not only are there multiple kinds of schools, colleges and universities, but the system is riddled with contradictions and inexorably intertwined with education experiences that stretch back many centuries. In England, we have some of the oldest formal Learning Organisations anywhere in the world. The majority were created by wealthy benefactors who wanted to share their wealth and experience by helping to educate the next generation. The majority of those organisations are now fee paying rather than supported by state funding. These organisations have long histories, stretching back to pre-industrial ages. Looking at schools for young people aged between five and eighteen for example, there are nine original charitable schools that were set up by wealthy benefactors, often with support from the church. All of them are now global brands that are synonymous with high-quality learning. Of these, Westminster is the oldest, tracing its roots back to 1179. The others are Winchester College founded in 1324, Eton College founded in 1440, Shrewsbury School founded in 1552, Harrow School founded in 1572, Rugby School founded in 1567, Charterhouse School founded in 1611, St Paul's School founded in 1509 and Merchant Taylors' School founded in 1561 – the latter two being day schools whilst the others are boarding schools. In their original forms, these schools were male only and selected those with the necessary ability to fill their places. Other very successful fee-paying schools emerged over time. These organisations appear to have significantly skewed the view we have of education. They are very successful, they nurture their pupils and create a broad social context around which they deliver their learning. The students that emerge from these organisations are literate, numerate and well-rounded individuals. Therefore, of those that actually attended full-time education, the outcome was a high-quality output of learners that exhibited all the attributes we hear being talked about. But the point is that this was a small proportion of the population. If we add to this mix that for a very long time a large majority of our senior politicians in England have been fortunate enough to have experienced this kind of learning environment, then we begin to perhaps see how the myth around what an education system should provide has developed. Again, I would stress that this aspiration is totally laudable and one that we should all aspire to, but the way it is achieved for this small percentage of the population is not transferable to the population as a whole.

As we look across the spectrum of Learning Organisations we see many models emerging that differ significantly from the model described above. Some are being driven by business entrepreneurs who often come from a social background that has denied them access to the system described above. So, over time, we have created a schism – if that is not too strong a word. On the one hand, we have an enviable tradition of scholarship that runs back to the earliest times where the (mostly) male children of wealthy individuals were able to access learning of the highest quality. Over the years these organisations have developed and shaped themselves with the times and still hold the highest reputation both in this country and abroad. Most now educate girls as well as boys, although some are still single sex and most have updated and invested in their facilities so that they are the envy of all who visit them. Compare this to the revolution that was brought about by a series of acts of parliament in Britain that led to the provision of free education for all children. The key acts were the 1880 Elementary Education Act that made it law for all five to ten year olds to attend school, the Balfour Act of 1902 that set up Local Education Authorities, the Fisher Act of 1918 that made education compulsory up to the age of fourteen and the 1944 Butler Education Reform Act that set up a tripartite system in England. These acts of parliament laid the changes that have enabled young people to have access to a broad range of learning up to and beyond degree level.

The challenge in our system is that the learning experiences of many very influential individuals have been shaped by this landscape of elite fee-paying schools. These high-achieving individuals have flourished and benefited from this particular form of learning. Their experience creates a utopian view, as I touched on earlier, where everyone is literate and numerate and where summative exams are the critical benchmark. Their view is one that cannot easily be dismissed because unless you are *very* careful and *very* adept at debating you can end up appearing, or be cast as appearing, to argue against high levels of literacy and numeracy. I believe that we need to recognise that this particular 'recipe' for learning is unique; it fulfils a purpose and sets a standard but is not completely representative of our broad society or representative of what our economy can afford for every learner. Firstly, this model is based on selection and in a universal education system you fundamentally cannot select pupils, as everyone is entitled to get an education. Secondly, it is expensive. The funding model for fee-paying education sets the bar too high for all but the top few per cent of earners in society. And thirdly, it is elitist by its very nature because of the cost and the selection criteria. None of the things this model represents is wrong in itself and the model provides something that many countries and systems aspire to replicate. But we do create a false 'yardstick' against which to judge our Learning Organisations in general. And this judgement clouds all of our thinking. It creates false views on how learning should be delivered, it creates false views on how we should measure success and it creates a model against which few, if any, state-funded organisations can ever hope to measure up against if they aspire to educate every learner.

This might all sound defeatist but it is the reality. At the extreme end of the spectrum we minimise the achievements of learners who explore ideas and topics that are not in the mainstream. We risk losing the opportunities to look at new ways of exploring ideas and we lock our Learning Organisations into a pre-industrial view of learning that then becomes the norm against which to measure all Learning Organisations. As a society, we risk not celebrating excellence in all its forms and instead celebrate a narrow band of excellence that is relevant to some but not to the majority of learners in our ever-broadening social mix.

What is the reaction to the unstoppable change we are seeing? The majority of people are comfortable with the status quo. Change is hard, change is disruptive and, therefore, many of us avoid change. But change is inevitable and cannot be stopped. The very nature of experimenting and finding things out leads to change and makes us look for new experiences. In my experience, it is those that are proactive about change that reap the benefits. But what if you can't make sense of the changes that are happening? What if the change is so at odds with your experiences that it is completely disorientating and appears to break some of the truths that you held to be constant? History is full of such stories, from the denial by the early Christian church that the earth was not the centre of the universe to the revelations from the Large Hadron Collider.

Until the advent of the Smart device it was pretty hard to make audio and video recordings. Cameras have been around for a long time so taking pictures was relatively easy, although the instant image sharing that Smart devices enables has redefined the way pictures are used. In 2016 about 1 billion pictures were taken and stored. Creating and sharing text has been relatively easy since the invention of the printing press in the 1640s. Because our current education systems are predominantly rooted in the industrial era, the only accepted form of assessment appears to be to get learners to write things down. Text was the primary means of communication in the industrial era and, therefore, our education systems were of course predicated in writing. Somehow, using audio and video is looked upon as a secondary and less intellectual way of sharing your learning in our education systems. However, last time I looked the film industry was a globally important industry and those who make great films are heralded as important storytellers. With the Oscars, BAFTAs and a myriad of other major award ceremonies celebrating the art of filmmaking, clearly we value those who can tell a story using video. Similarly, high-quality documentary films are seen as a critical part of what public broadcasters provide for the licence fee they collect from the taxpayer, and advertiser-funded content similarly sees value in these formats. So why do we not support our learners to use video as a legitimate means of telling us what they have learnt?

Audio is used extensively via radio, and now via online streaming, to tell important stories. Flagship radio stations like the BBC World Service and BBC Radio 4 share critical and important stories, from breaking news to documentary. So why do we not support our learners to use audio as a legitimate means of telling us what they have learnt? Photojournalism has been used to tell the world about some of the most important stories in history – from the earliest pioneers like Ansel Adams who raised awareness of environmental issues, to the heartbreaking image of the young Syrian boy who was found dead on a beach in Greece in late 2015. So why do we not support our learners to use images as a legitimate mainstream means of telling what they have learnt?

In all this we really do get to a key point in understanding how far removed from a post-industrial 21st-century education system we really are. In none of this am I in any way intimating that learning to read and write are not important. Text and cursive writing is and will remain an essential part of any education system. Writing books, writing articles and writing plays and scripts are essential for a modern society. But in the industrial age we stopped just there, because getting access to the tools to make high-quality images, audio recordings and films was either non-existent or prohibitively expensive. Even if you could get the equipment, and some organisations did find the funding, learning the skills to operate the equipment took too much time to allow their effective use or would cost too much in salaries to employ the people with the necessary skills.

Thus, in the industrial age we inadvertently created a 'Taxonomy of Smartness' that has embedded itself in society and is the basis of the education systems we see in operation today. The taxonomy lists, in order of 'smartness', the skills an individual needs to master to be judged as successful and to access our current education systems.

The taxonomy is, in effect, also a series of 'gates' through which learners need to pass to be seen as successful. The taxonomy is as follows:

1   The creation and manipulation of text. This includes a complex series of rules that dictate what individuals must be able to do at a certain age. Much of this is causing significant controversy as I write this text, as the formulaic nature of the guidance appears to be at odds with the current use of language. There are many more better qualified than me to argue the case, but in this context the formulaic nature of the guidance appears to be somewhat behind the times when compared to current vernacular language use. But, if you can master text then you are smart and you might be able to go and look at the following list items, if there is time.

2   The creation and manipulation of images. Drawing has been taught in education systems for many years, but with the dawn of the post-industrial age the ability to take images and to then manipulate those images using digital techniques has become as simple and easy as writing text. As photojournalism shows, the use of an image can be powerful and create a legitimate way of sharing understanding and insight.

3   The creation and manipulation of audio. Constructing and managing the delivery of an audio story requires significant skills and understanding, from how to pace delivery to how to build an effective script. Storytelling through oral communication is a skill that goes back as far as we can see in history. Before writing and reading, storytellers used the audio medium to share ideas with local communities.

4   The creation and manipulation of video. We often think of this as high-end and complex. The medium was previously dominated by expensive production processes and the need for complex equipment. With the advent of YouTube and other video-sharing sites, and with the inclusion of video cameras on Smart devices, the process has been democratised. There are many examples of mostly young people producing video vignettes that are insightful and well produced. These are produced for small capital outlay and attract billions of views. The reaction I mostly get to this discussion is that the content is not worthy or that it is subversive. Check out Dan TDM on YouTube. Check out his sold-out world tour and then his book . . . you just might spot something revolutionary.

So, we judge that if you can't produce high-quality text then you should not progress through the taxonomy, and if you can't produce high-quality text then you are somehow less worthy. Eventually this becomes a hierarchy that bars entry to anyone who cannot operate successfully in the world of written text. In his book *Before Writing*, Gunther Kress has some fascinating insights into the way we learn to read and decode text.[5] He uses examples of children drawing images and shows how those images then form into text. In his book *The Symbolic Species*, Terrence Deacon also explores the nature of our species in terms of imagery.[6] It turns out that language is, in effect, a series of elaborate images that have become stylised to become language and that textual language has then been used to create written representations of sound. We are, therefore, inexorably visual and auditory beings that have created a complex symbolic system to represent the things we've been talking about, singing about and drawing about since we first started to communicate with each other. Thus, to create an industrial education system that positively discriminates against image, audio and video appears to be bizarre. Many have argued similar things from a variety of standpoints. This focus on textual representation has been seen as removing from our education systems a wide range of creative subjects. This argument has been made eloquently in audio and video by Ken Robinson in his animated talk for the Royal Society of Arts (RSA).[7]

Therefore, we can possibly think of a new way to understand and interpret learning. Why shouldn't we turn the taxonomy on its head and allow learners to explore learning by using video, audio and imagery tools, with those tools given equal weight as the use and manipulation of text. If an example were needed, listen to the podcast at the following link: https://soundcloud.com/the-show-about-science. The young person doing the questioning is clearly at ease exploring the world in audio using verbal skills to learn and understand the world around him.

I can almost hear those in the establishment groaning at the some of these statements and the exploration of anything that is not rooted in the belief that literacy is the only foundation for success. I've stated several times in this book that I believe we need to make sure that our learners have the basic elements of literacy and numeracy and that they master these elements. But these are no longer the only elements that learners need. We all need to master and understand how the tools we have at our fingertips can be used to our personal and professional advantage. We can't simply stop the world in the mid-1990s and pretend that none of the technological developments has taken place. To do so is not only silly, it is to betray the young learners that are coming through our system. It is a false dawn to turn our backs on anything but literacy, declaring that this is the only valid foundation that our learners need to be successful.

Notes

1 Schleicher, A. (2015). *Students, Computers and Learning: Making the Connection*. Paris: PISA, OECD Publishing.
2 *Ibid.*, Page 3.
3 Bradley, S. (2015). *The Railways: Nation, Network and People.* London: Profile Books Ltd.
4 Schleicher, *op. cit.* (note 1).
5 Kress, G. (1997). *Before Writing*. London: Routledge.
6 Deacon, T. (1997). *The Symbolic Species.* London: Allen Lane, The Penguin Press Ltd.
7 Robinson, K. (2010). Changing Education Paradigms. Available at: https://youtube/zDZFcDGpL4U [2017].

7 Myths and legends overcoming prejudice

Technology and learning

Myths and legends have been around since the dawn of time. They are made up of stories that have their origins in some grain of truth or some idea that began circulating and was taken as being true. Often the idea gets handed down from generation to generation, with each generation adding a bit of embellishment until the original grain of truth gets buried deep beneath the rich tapestry of the story. And so it is with technology in education. As I talk with learners, teachers and senior leaders, some consistent themes emerge that move across organisational boundaries and across organisations themselves. The themes appear in conversations with higher education, further education and under-eighteen education organisations. These topics concern the application of technology to learning and are more often than not used by many to justify not integrating technology into the fabric of their organisation. I've characterised these themes as the 'myths and legends' that are shared about the role of technology in education systems. These myths and legends, often in the form of broad statements, hide fertile areas for discussion and, as with all myths and legends, they contain a grain of truth that warrants further exploration. I've shared my top-ten myths and legends below and for each I've shared a short narrative of the circumstances in which they appear. Also, for each of the myths and legends I've highlighted the grain of truth that sits at the heart of the 'myth' that often gets lost as the myth develops.

Myth #1: technology has not changed anything

There are still many involved in education who will defend this statement, and on one level I agree with them. Let me explain. Learning itself is timeless as I've discussed in other chapters of the book. And for some the model for an education system has altered very little for centuries. The traditional class or lecture-room model where subjects are taught to groups of broadly same-age peers persists and continues to be successful. So, from that perspective working with a group of people in a face-to-face environment has not changed and technology has done little if anything to significantly erode this mode. In this context, high-quality teachers remain the essential ingredient and always will be until the end of time. Add a layer of high-quality leadership to support, challenge and develop teachers and great Learning Organisations emerge. With these prerequisites in place then a logically defensible position can be adopted that technology had not changed anything. Indeed, many argue, as Schleicher does, that technology can actively get in the way of face-to-face interaction, diluting the power of the teacher: students paying more attention to their mobile device than to the teacher; using devices to secretly video the teacher or to communicate with their peers rather than focusing on the activities in the lesson. All these activities can be seen as subverting the flow of a lecture or lesson.

But there are profound changes taking place in society. The ubiquitous nature of technology and the 'App for Everything' culture is defining the way we interact with a whole range of services. We can't access money, travel or communicate over distances without technology. From the fixed-line telephone to the 'Smart' device, our societies are evolving rapidly. And, likewise, in classrooms and lecture rooms across the world a quiet revolution is taking place – a revolution in the way that teachers are choosing to interact with students. High-quality teachers have always, and will always, adapt the way they interact with students. Anyone who has spent time in a classroom knows that every group of students is different. Individual characters can take lessons in one direction whilst another group will pull discussions subtly into another direction. So, teachers constantly adapt what they do; not to the extent that learning objectives are compromised, but always to take account of the dynamics of the specific groups of learners. By the nature of the vocation, teachers want to do the best for all their students.

Our high-quality teaching force is adopting technology in exciting and new ways. They are adapting their practices, and they are clinically looking at technology and applying it to improve interactions with their students. However, because this is happening quietly in Learning

Organisations across the land, within the learning environment the perception is that nothing has changed and that change is still not happening. So, the grain of truth in this first myth is that nothing has changed. The face-to-face interaction with a high-quality 'teacher' is the most powerful way for learning to happen. But within this lies the desire for these 'teachers' to use the best possible tools to support their teaching – in there sits the profound change. Teachers are adopting and adapting the best tools to support great learning, but at the system level this is not being acknowledged or leveraged.

Myth #2: technology makes no difference

If nothing has changed then clearly technology is making no difference. As we've explored with Myth #1, things are changing and technology is making a difference. It's how you define the difference that is important. Education measures success by outcomes and against end-of-module, term, year or stage tests. The temptation is to try and quantify how the application of technology to learning has improved those outcomes. I think the only analogy I can make here is with journalism. Has the mass adoption of Twitter made journalists better in any many measurable way? Probably not. In fact, with the initial 140-character limit for messages on Twitter one could argue that it has diluted the journalist's art, forcing complex stories to be stripped back to sensational headlines and forcing contractions to words (e.g. 'great' becomes 'gr8') that break grammatical conventions. However, what it has done is allowed news items to be shared quickly, allowed the contemporaneous voice of people at the heart of a situation to be heard and spread ideas far beyond traditional boundaries. Journalism has adapted to take advantage of this explosion in 'social media' and used it to shape stories faster and in real time.

If education starts and ends at the doors of a classroom and is measured in specific time periods then the potential to interact with students beyond that clearly delineated world is limited. As a great teacher, you might use technology as we explored in Myth #1, but stop there, keeping learning within the walls of your lecture or classroom and using technology more as a personal enabler. You will set homework that your students do outside the classroom but, mostly, the expectation is that this work will be done solely by the student and presented to the teacher for marking.

If your learning world does not stop at the classroom door and is not completely bound by a timeslot then how do you interact with your students? Enter technology in many forms. From social media to collaborative online environments, technology has stepped up to make that interaction possible, meaningful and worthwhile. Just as in the journalism example, brief interactions between students and teachers can support significant additional understanding. In the area of 'beyond the classroom' technology, savvy teachers are using tools to support learners to go further, move faster and become smarter.

But what about in that classroom space where teacher and learner interact in a deep learning conversation? Is technology of no use there? In the hands of a good teacher these tools can revolutionise the way learning can be shared. And these tools are changing the learning landscape. We often focus on the learners using the tools, and justifiably so as many can find ways of expressing themselves through these mediums that feel natural to them. But high-quality teachers are adopting the technology to hone and share their learning messages.

So, the grain of truth in this myth is that technology itself makes no difference, but in the hands of a highly skilled educator it can make their teaching more powerful and take on greater significance to a broader range of learners – overall outcomes arguably improve as the messages from the teacher strike home to a wider range of their learners.

Myth #3: learning has not changed

This one is a bit trickier! But discussions around technology often justifiably move into discussions around how people, notably the young, 'learn differently'. If we start with the grain of truth in this myth then maybe we can explore better why some people think learning *has* changed.

Most definitions of learning are linked to the acquisition of knowledge, facts or understanding. But we constantly hear that employers are looking for more than just the ability to recite facts and knowledge, especially in the post-industrial age that we now inhabit. The ability to collaborate, communicate effectively and share knowledge are cited as important skills. Areas of mathematics and science have now become so complex that no one person can solve the next set of problems. There are so many patents and claims to intellectual property (IP) lodged across multiple legal jurisdictions that understanding if your 'new idea' is

Knowledge
v
Skills

really new becomes a significant challenge. Collaboration and sharing become essential skills. Researching online databases also becomes essential, and sifting fact from opinion and speculation becomes a critical skill. Where previously the power of the individual was key, now the power of a collective is needed to solve the next set of big problems. And so the human species is set on a course to build and create the tools that will support this need to collaborate and share.

What we need to learn and how we can acquire that knowledge has changed. There are new ways of acquiring and accessing knowledge. Do different generations learn differently? Is the pen mightier than the tablet? Having access to resources that are shared on the World Wide Web allows learners to explore ideas and topics in ways that were impossible twenty years ago. Does this change the nature of learning? If I no longer need to remember a set of numbers or tracts of text because I can access them at will on a device, does this change the way I learn?

So, at one level, learning has not changed and technology has done nothing to change learning. However, the potential methods of acquiring knowledge have changed. The change in the method of acquisition of knowledge frames the discussion about whether learning has changed. Some things that once had to be remembered can now easily be accessed using personal mobile technology. There is the now-famous comment that teachers made in the 1990s that you would not always have a calculator to hand so mental maths was essential. Anyone with a mobile phone, and that's around 4.9 billion[1] of us as I write today, walks around with a powerful calculator.

I believe that the lines are not clearly drawn. Does the act of learning by rote have merit, even though a device can be used to instantly recall a fact, a sequence of numbers or carry out a mathematical calculation in the modern world? Clearly there is a need for skills in collaboration and sharing. If you have not worked with someone on a collaborative document then the experience is very different from emailing copies back and forth and using tracked changes. There is a skill set that needs to be explored – a skill set that is different and one that needs overt development.

The synthesis of existing knowledge to create new insights is clearly a 21st-century reality, although even in the 1700s Isaac Newton commented famously: '*If I have seen further than others, it is by standing upon the shoulders of giants.*' It is not an 'accident' that the protocols that drive the World Wide Web were created by Tim Berners-Lee to support research scientists to share their knowledge at the CERN particle research facility. It was clear that the complexity of the ideas being researched demanded the collaboration of experts from many domains.

If this sounds like a niche for the scientific elite then it is not. All public services in the UK are being referenced and supported by online materials using the gov.net platform. The expectation is that this platform will be the first point of contact between the citizen and government. This means that the ability to effectively access and use online platforms will be a necessity for *every citizen*. This is not a singular trend in one country. Every nation state is looking to place services on to these platforms, making the skills required to access and understand the collaborative online world non-negotiable and essential.

Education has to change if we are to equip citizens to engage with the world. As I will discuss in the next myth, a personal device, therefore, takes on more significance than just being a nice 'extra' to have.

Myth #4: having a personal device makes no difference

Building on the Myth #3, it is clear that having a personal device can make a difference. Whether that difference is considered to have value is the critical question. If learning is framed along very traditional lines then the grain of truth in this myth is that a personal device makes little or no difference. If access to the device is restricted within the learning environment then it cannot be of any use or make any difference. If the nature of assessment is focused on summative examinations that measure the individual then having a device makes little or no difference.

In an education system, where learning is defined as knowing things, being able to recall facts and quote agreed and sanctioned texts, and where testing is summative and individualised, then personal devices will make no tangible difference. However, in an education system where knowledge is valued and where collaboration is valued, where formative assessment is used as a benchmark as well as summative assessment and where complex shared problem solving is encouraged, then personal devices will make a difference. They are essential in this model. Accessing a wide variety of source material, debating, sharing insights and sharing personal understanding become tangible and sought-after skills; accessing materials quickly and effectively also becomes a sought-after skill.

There is a very good case to be made that post-industrial societies are at this point already. The skills and attributes listed in the previous paragraph are exactly what employers are looking for. The mismatch between these two positions on its own defines the problems with current education systems in my view. To succeed in society, people need to communicate. In an industrial age, that was done with letters and latterly with fixed telephone systems. But with the advent of the mobile phone and smartphone the model of exchanging letters and the occasional phone call has been blown apart. This traditional model is so broken that if we were to start trying to converse by letter then we would be at a significant disadvantage in so many ways. Think about running your business, your personal life and your financial affairs using traditional letters and the surface mail system. I predict that less than twenty-four hours into trying to do this you would lose patience and revert to electronic tools and use your personal device.

So why do we persist in promulgating these practices in our education system? I am not an advocate for 'not learning to write longhand' as there are still occasions when we need to pick up a pen, although the only thing I remember using a pen for recently was to sign official documents. Cursive writing and having legible handwriting is important but not to the degree that was the case in an industrial society. In the pre-industrial age, writing and literacy were the preserve of the few as there was little need for writing or reading when the sole occupation was labouring or working on the land. During the industrial age, these skills of literacy and numeracy became the hallmarks of being educated. Those who were educated with these skills were able to build a lifestyle to which many aspired and a significant number of those who had made great fortunes on the back of industrialisation felt the need to give back to society through philanthropic gestures, many of which were targeted at education. If we switch our model to a post-industrial one then not having access to a personal device will become as much a disadvantage as not being literate and numerate were in the industrial era.

Myth #5: ignore the Internet because it is not safe

For the technology experts reading this I've deliberately used the word 'Internet'. In colloquial language, the Internet and the Web are used synonymously; they are, in fact, two distinct things. The Internet is the wires, fibres and cables that connect servers and computers to each other. The Internet has existed since the early 1970s when universities and the military recognised that the ability to share data across the world instantly provided significant advantage. The World Wide Web is a set of protocols that were conceived and honed by the CERN community led by Tim Berners-Lee. The Web is the revolution that makes the sharing of ideas, documents and other digital artefacts possible for the general public. Berners-Lee defined the protocols in the early 1990s and thereby laid the foundations for Google to be born in 1998. Initially set up to provide a way of searching the exponential growth in content on the Web, Google have gone on to help redefine the way we share and collaborate in the digital domain. Google Apps (G Suite) and YouTube serve billions of users. Other tech companies have of course exploited the Web. Both Apple and Microsoft who were founded in the mid-1970s quickly began to develop their offerings to take advantage of the collaborative possibilities of the Web.

The way Berners-Lee conceived the Web was to make it open to all. In the spirit of academic freedom, the protocols were made open to everyone and the adoption was swift and has redefined the world we now inhabit. But therein lies the challenge. Because it was open to all, literally anyone was able to create content and make it accessible to anyone else. This attracted the good and, let's be frank, it also attracted 'the bad'. The technology itself is neither good nor bad. The use to which it is put by individuals and groups is the real challenge.

The grain of truth in this myth is that there are areas of the Web that need to be ignored – areas and spaces that have been created by individuals or groups that have a particular agenda. In the late 1990s and early 2000s I worked with IBM looking at the rise of the Web in education. We concluded then that educators needed to take control of how and when resources are used. Educators and our education systems should take advantage of the opportunities for sharing and group work, but in a way that makes learners aware of the challenges and opportunities. The Web is no different to every other walk of life. There are those who would seek to create advantage through being less than honest and there are places and areas that we would actively seek to stop young learners looking. Simply ignoring the Web or shying away from using the positive aspects is not tenable and is certainly not an excuse for ignoring the many positive benefits.

Myth #6: children know more about tech than adults

I like this myth because it gets to the heart of a number of critical issues about the role of technology not only in education but in the wider world. The grain of truth in this myth is that children explore and experiment in ways that adults appear to have forgotten. The natural curiosity of childhood demands that exploring things and finding out how things work is a critical attribute of the young. So, in embarking on exploration, 'fiddling' with things and generally trying to find out how things work means that young people consistently appear to understand the technology better than adults. This is good, in that they appear proficient, but bad because many adults find it intimidating that the young people they are meant to be teaching know more than they do. This speaks to the industrial model for education, where the teacher was the expert and, because of age and advantage, was assumed to know more than the learner and was recognised as being the domain expert.

In the modern world, no one can know everything about a topic or area. There will of course always be domain experts who have concentrated on understanding an area or topic to a level of expertise that few other can hope to achieve. As we move on in our growth as a species we understand more about the way our world works. As Figure 7.1 shows,[2] in 1900 we knew of roughly 80 elements; now we know of nearly 120.

Simply remembering facts and ideas is becoming more and more impossible as the sum total of knowledge grows. So, we need to have new ways of accessing facts and knowledge.

I would develop this myth further to say that really understanding the potential for technology in education is not well understood or well documented anywhere in the world. We are still at a stage where enthusiastic individuals are evangelising about the power and potential of technology in learning. There are literally thousands of new education technology sites and resources being created each year. We are in a wonderful period of experimentation. The focus always ends up with the device and not on the pedagogy, and in those circumstances the students do end up knowing more about the device than the adults do. It is time to really understand the role of these devices in learning (I will comment more on this later).

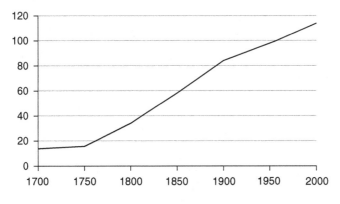

Figure 7.1 Number of known chemical elements 1700–2000.

Myth #7: physical buildings are the centre of learning

If we refer back to our myth about learning not having changed and we define Learning Organisations and education from an industrial standpoint, then physical buildings are certainly the focal point for learning. Therein lies the grain of truth in this myth. Even the most radical education reform programmes are still focusing on building new school buildings, college campuses and university campuses or creating physical spaces where learners must congregate for a set number of hours per week. There have been a number of 'Classroom of the Future' projects globally, with funding to look at design, and within the Building Schools for the Future Programme in England there certainly were some excellent and not so excellent new learning buildings built. However, the costs of these programmes inevitably exceed the available public funding and they inevitably stop before they can be fully explored.

I recently talked to a principal and assistant principal who had created a 'pop-up' school in an unused building on the outskirts of London. They are not the first to try this idea. As they described this project we began to unpick what was really needed to build a great Learning Organisation. Whilst the physical space is important, the essence of the organisation exists in the people and not the physical space. Elsewhere I have referenced research that looked at what makes highly effective schools. Of eleven characteristics, the research does cite an orderly atmosphere as being important for an attractive working environment.

But this does not have to mean that buildings need to cost millions or even be specially designed. I think education has a lot to learn from retail. In retail environments, generic spaces are used and within those spaces specific environments are created. As you wander around a large department store, a well-known Swedish home-furnishings store comes to mind here, but there are others: you are transported from one setting to another where micro-environments are created with the minimum of fuss and at quite a low cost compared to commissioning bespoke buildings. Learning Organisations do have specialised areas, but then so do these stores. Most have some kind of eating facilities and areas where customers pay and collect goods. The other feature of these buildings is that they all have Wi-Fi by default. As President Obama famously said in early 2014, specifically about the US: *'In a country where we expect free WiFi with our coffee, we should definitely demand it in our schools.'*[3] If technology systems are considered at the design stage of our learning systems, then physical buildings need no longer be the only place where learning can take place. The nature of physical buildings used for learning can change, they can become less expensive, they can become grounded in the centre of communities, they can be flexed and change as our society develops and changes. They can also grow to serve learners from three to twenty-three just by using more of the space that may be sitting around and underused, just as the profile of retail shifts. I've made references to this in two further places in this book: in an article that I have included called 'No Classroom Required' and in Chapter 4 where I look at the nature of learning spaces in general.

Myth #8: search engines replace the need to know things

This is one of those myths that very quickly gets transformed into a high-stakes political debate. Before we succumb to that debate, let's look at the facts. If I have a device and a good Wi-Fi connection then it is quicker and easier to search for something electronically than using a library. I don't prescribe to the debate that you can't trust online searches. Any decent education system helps learners to understand the difference between fact and opinion and there are trusted sources on the Web in exactly the same way as there are trusted published resources.

But does the ability to search for things replace the need to know things? No. It is still important for people to know things, but I think that misses the point. In some way those who are against technology present searching as somehow lazy and this is where the debate becomes politicised in my view. If our young people – and this myth is mostly aimed at the young – simply type in a word to a search engine and get a response then they somehow become lazy and their learning somehow becomes less worthy.

Deep subject-based knowledge is essential and still needs to be taught. But the ability to use online tools to update facts and explore further to look at new research and new ideas is an essential skill in the 21st century. Search engines augment our knowledge and expertise. They can provide access to additional knowledge and new ideas that would previously not have been accessible.

Myth #9: the technology industry can be trusted to look after edtech

Having spent a good deal of time working in and around the technology industry, as well as in education systems, this is a myth I feel well qualified to discuss. My answer is . . . 'No'! This is normally a myth put about by the technology companies to allow them to present a particular piece of hardware or software as the answer to everyone's woes.

But there is a balance to be struck here. That balance is between the need to engage with those developing the new hardware and software and those engaged in the learning process. There needs to be a much closer relationship between educators and technology companies. I referenced elsewhere in this book that I would draw more comparisons between the way technology is developing for healthcare and how technology needs to develop for education. Education technology is too reliant on consumer technology. There are very few technology companies who have dedicated education research and development units. Mostly, they have people looking at how their consumer devices can be repurposed for education. There are some exceptions, but these tend to be in areas where specific software is required, like management information systems. Some companies like Google have developed specific software for education to be completely fair about this. But the challenge then comes when Learning Organisations want to mix and match ecosystems. The lack of impartial advice leads to the 'one solution will solve all your problems' approach, which is not the case.

There needs to be more global, national and local consultation between teachers and tech companies. This needs to be beyond the level of sponsorship where products and services are promoted in return for support or equipment. There is no 'agnostic' global institute for education technology, probably due to the underlying theme of this book – in our predominantly industrial education models we are struggling to recognise the power of technology.

Myth #10: leave them alone and it will all be OK

This myth grows from the idea that young people have some inbuilt understanding of how technology works. I do not believe this to be true. What the young have that older generations have perhaps forgotten is the urge to 'tinker', to try things out. As the 'Hole in the Wall' experiments by Sugatra Mitra showed, children will find out how things work.[4] They will tinker until they spot patterns and from there work out the rules of the game. From there they will work out how things work, and subsequently they will be more than happy to share with peers and others how they have mastered the new idea, tool or gizmo. There's nothing new there really – it is what the human species has been doing for thousands of years. It is what has got us to where we are in our evolutionary journey. But is that enough? Should we just leave them alone? Possibly not.

One of the joys of teaching is to challenge learners to look at things from different perspectives and to challenge them to look for new ideas in familiar topics and ideas. As a colleague once said, our job is to challenge and support in equal measure. With that challenge and support comes a duty to guide learners to broader and deeper understandings. In the post-industrial era that job extends to challenging and supporting learners to use technology effectively, responsibly and to the greatest effect. As individuals, we don't need to know how things work to use them effectively. Few of us understand how a car works but we use them to get from one place to another. We are familiar enough with a simple set of controls to drive the car with confidence and safety. The same applies to our 21st-century tools. Learning how they work is arguably less important than using them to assist us with our learning. In a conversation with a senior leader in a school, he was telling me how he had shown his students in his English class the best way to email a professor at a university to get some guidance on what texts could support the book they were studying. The students got a reply, the recommended texts were ordered through an online book store and arrived within a few hours of the whole process being kicked off. The power of the tools being guided by the teacher significantly enhanced the learning, and along the way students picked up additional skills on how to elicit responses from academia and how the technology eco-system can be used to create significant value for the organisation. However, with this particular myth I sometimes think there is a deeper issue at play here. Sometimes I think part of the rationale is that by leaving the learners alone they might not understand the full potential of the technology and that in some ways it can then be trivialised and ignored. One example that comes to mind is a discussion with a senior educator in response to the following statement in a report I wrote in 2014:

> It is not possible to imagine a modern school or learning organisation without technology . . . we must be ambitious for our learners, provide them with the most powerful ways to learn and support them to be fully equipped for the 21st century.[5]

The discussion revolved around imagining a modern Learning Organisation without technology. At the pedagogical level, I can see the argument being defensible, but looking at the back-office systems, I'm not quite sure how that would work. Without technology there would be no email, no spreadsheets to analyse performance, no basic administration functions would operate so there would be no funding from government, and that's before we look at the classroom. Even the most technologically challenged Learning Organisations have some kind of presentation system in their teaching rooms and they are linked to computers of some kind. The discussion was within a broader context so the statement was part of a more complex argument. However, I cannot at this point in time think of any organisation that can function without some level of technology.

Let's deal with the prejudice

In all these myths and legends there is also a thread running through that has a hint of prejudice. It's as if there is a constant need to defend the place of technology in our education systems. The discussion starts from a position of defence rather than from the position of informed dialogue. Why is this the case? Maybe it is to do with the overwhelming desire to keep the status quo, as discussed earlier. To admit that technology is part of the way forward is to begin to recognise that the industrial model is no longer relevant. As we'll see in Chapter 8, technology can and should be taken for granted and fully embedded into a reformed system.

Notes

1 Statista.com. (2016). Mobile Phone Users Worldwide 2013–2019. Available at: www.statista.com/statistics/274774/forecast-of-mobile-phone-users-world-wide/ [2017].
2 Wikipedia. (2017). Timeline of Chemical Element Discoveries. Available at: https://en.wikipedia.org/wiki/Timeline_of_chemical_element_discoveries [2017].
3 *CBS News*. (2014). Obama: We Should Demand WiFi in Our Schools. Available at: www.cbsnews.com/news/obama-we-should-demand-wifi-in-our-schools/ [2017].
4 Edutopia. (2012). The Hole in the Wall Project and the Power of Self-Organized Learning. Available at: www.edutopia.org/blog/self-organized-learning-sugata-mitra [2017].
5 Penny, J. et al. (2014). Technology in Education: A System View. Available at: www.ednfoundation.org/wp-content/uploads/TechnologyEducation_system-view.pdf [2017].

8 What about the technology?

In this chapter, I want to look at how and where technology is really being used to make a difference in Learning Organisations. In the industrial age, the simple truth was that cause and effect was paramount, especially when looking at investment. In education, there are some very clear sets of evidence that point towards the things a system can do that will make a difference, but as we move further into the post-industrial age simple cause and effect is harder to pin down. There are still those who believe that global warming is not caused by burning fossil fuel, pointing to a raft of other reasons for the rise in average global temperatures. I am not an expert in climate science but certainly when you start to examine the evidence it becomes very complicated very quickly. Interpreting significant amounts of data, allowing for annual fluctuations and other variables creates a complex model that inevitably opens itself up to interpretation. So it is with learning and education systems. There are a considerable number of variables that come together in complex patterns that have an effect on learning outcomes. As a side note, I do not prescribe to the view that global warming is not man-made. It is clear from the evidence in my opinion that carbon emissions from burning fossil fuels are playing a significant factor in the rise of average global temperatures.

Those who look for a direct causal relationship between expenditure on technology in education and improved outcomes are deliberately or otherwise seeking to distort the overall picture. The 2015 OECD book *Students, Computers and Learning* is more interesting for what it says in the Foreword than for what the rest of the book covers. The book looks at the current state of education systems and finds that technology makes little impact. But, if you consider the fact that models for education systems are predominantly industrial then, as I've argued earlier, the impact of technology is minimal. In the Foreword, Andreas

What about the technology?

Schleicher makes several very important observations. Following comments about the lack of impact of technology, he says 'One interpretation of all this is that building deep, conceptual understanding and higher-order thinking requires intensive teacher-student interactions, and technology sometimes distracts from this valuable engagement'.[1]

I've related my thoughts on this in Myth #1, Chapter 7. However, he goes on to say 'Another interpretation is that we have not yet become good enough at the kind of pedagogies that make the most of technology; that adding 21st-century technologies to 20th century teaching practices will just dilute the effectiveness of teaching'.

In just a few paragraphs Schleicher writes passionately about some of the possibilities he sees and some of the challenges. He says 'The impact of technology on educational delivery remains sub-optimal, because we may overestimate the digital skills of both teachers and students, because of naive policy design and implementation strategies, because of poor quality educational software and courseware'.[2]

I covered this in Myths #6 and #9 (Chapter 7). There is a need to create places where teachers and education leaders can explore technology and pedagogy, and this cannot be something that is funded by the technology industry. If it is, then it will simply reflect what the industry wants to sell and not what is really needed. As with medical research, the experts need to lead the commercial organisations to build and create what will make a real difference.

Schleicher also comments:

> We need to get this right in order to provide educators with learning environments that support 21st-century pedagogies and provide children with the 21st-century skills they need to succeed in tomorrow's world. Technology is the only way to dramatically expand access to knowledge.

I could quote the entire Foreword, but I would urge you to read the full text. The last piece I will include here is pertinent to the whole theme of this book:

> To deliver on the promise technology holds, countries will need a convincing strategy to build teachers' capacity. And policy-makers need to become better at building support for this agenda . . . . Last but not least, it is vital that teachers become active agents for change, not just implementing technological innovations, but in designing them too.

As I've commented earlier, teachers are leading the way, but this is not being supported anywhere near enough. We don't need traditional industrial-scale training programmes or complex national programmes that cost millions and take years to roll out. We need agile, short and snappy sessions that teachers can access as and when they need them. These need not be expensive to create or expensive to deliver.

Trying to hold back the tide

As the OECD and many others observe, mobile technology is dominating our societies. The number of devices are proliferating and the amount of data being downloaded is exploding. Young people are connected. They are accessing 'stuff' to support their learning. It makes sense to embrace and use personal mobile technology in our Learning Organisations.

As Figure 8.1 and Figure 8.2 show, the rise of mobile technology and use of data is growing very fast. The figures are taken from an organisation that represents the mobile phone companies and give a snapshot of how their businesses are developing. It is clear that the trend is unstoppable and that trying to deny the role that technology will play in learning is folly. Up-to-date data is provided by the GSMA – an organisation that represents the mobile operators. The latest trends are available at the GSMA website.[3] But let's not forget Schleicher's comment: ' . . . *countries will need a convincing strategy to build teachers' capacity and policy-makers need to become better at building support for this agenda'.*[4] So, what are the challenges that exist in integrating mobile technology into our current systems? What are the challenges in ensuring that technology in general is used to support high-quality learning and is not seen as a 'nice to have' option? The use of ICT in education has long been seen as making a significant difference to the learning process. Recently I asked a very successful principal of a high-performing school to tell me why she thought ICT was so important in her school.

She paused . . . and said, 'Imagine the school without ICT.' The point was well made – you simply cannot imagine a 21st-century Learning Organisation without ICT, it is inconceivable. From email to the phone system, the cashless catering systems, not to mention the equipment that teachers and learners use every day in lessons, ICT is quite simply an essential part of any school, university or Learning Organisation.

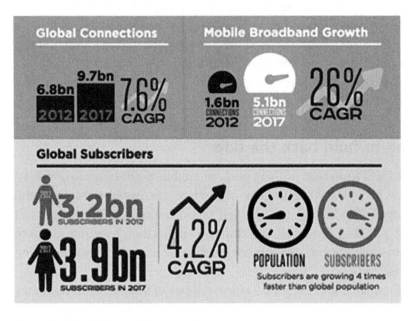

Figure 8.1 Growth in mobile connections.

Source: www.gsmaintelligence.com

However, ICT is *necessary but not sufficient* on its own. It is one of the tools that can be used to support and inspire learning.

But why are there still questions about exactly how ICT makes a difference to learning and how it should be deployed and used? There are quite significant differences between what very senior educators think ICT can bring to learning. Some are keen to use the latest mobile technology, three-dimensional (3D) simulations and push for innovation, talking of the transformation that ICT brings to the learning process. Others are clear that ICT is essential but that it need not be overly complex; it just needs to work in a reliable way and provide educators with a tool – in their view, well-implemented ICT is like the Stradivarius violin, it adds a unique quality to an already virtuoso performance.

I'd like to pose a question: What are the factors that make a school, a Learning Organisation or even a regional or national strategy successful and how can those factors be supported by ICT?

We'll take a look at this question in due course. We will also look at why the use of mobile devices in schools is still a controversial topic, with some organisations and systems having an outright ban whilst some actively encourage their usage.

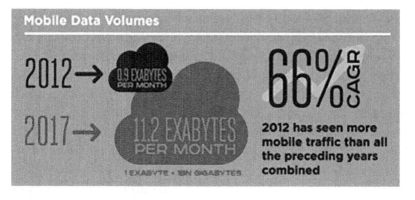

Figure 8.2 Growth in mobile data use.
Source: www.gsmaintelligence.com

Research

First let's look at some research. I'm always surprised at the number of people who talk about high-quality education that have not spent time looking at the literature on school effectiveness. Whilst it might at first look to be a complex field, there are a couple of important pieces of research that have stood the test of time and, like all really great insights, are as true today as they were when the research was undertaken. The simplest and most effective piece of research into effective Learning Organisations was undertaken in the early 1990s by a group of researchers at the Institute of Education, University of London. Interestingly, the research was commissioned by the relatively new organisation called the Office for Standards in Education (OFSTED). The researchers visited a number of schools considered to be highly effective in various countries and collated the common themes that they saw in each of them. They came up with eleven key characteristics of effectiveness. These are: professional leadership, shared vision and goals, the creation of a learning environment, a concentration on teaching and learning, purposeful teaching, setting of high expectations, positive reinforcement, effective monitoring of progress, the importance of pupil rights and responsibilities to raise self-esteem, the importance of home–school partnerships and an organisation that learns about having a clear approach to staff development.

Twenty years later and hundreds of visits to Learning Organisations later, I've yet to find any reason not to go back to this list and tick off each and every one of the factors as being present in a high-performing Learning Organisation. This research was embraced by several other countries who used the initial research to start to build improvement in their systems. The initial research was updated slightly and revised and found its way into a publication called *Perspectives on School Effectiveness and Improvement*, published in 1997.[5] This research not only went on to underpin some of the key pillars behind the National Professional Qualification for Headteachers (NPQH) in the late 1990s in England, but also formed the basis from which OFSTED has continued to build. The research is relatively easy to understand and creates a simple framework around which to build and then develop highly effective Learning Organisations. Interestingly, no further such research has been commissioned and none has been commissioned that looks at how technology supports highly effective Learning Organisations anywhere in the world. All research around technology and learning tries to create a direct link between expenditure and improvement.

Below I have created a table (see Table 8.1) that takes the slightly revised key characteristics identified in the research referenced above and adds a column that comments on the role of technology. It is clear to me that high-performing organisations are using technology to great effect. It's not looked at by OFSTED, or is very rarely commented upon by any inspection regime, but when used well technology is a very powerful tool that complements and underpins the way an organisation seeks to work to deliver great learning.

The table highlights that the possibilities in education are no different to the possibilities in any other business area. It is just that education is being very slow to change underlying processes to allow it to take advantage of the possibilities offered by technology. In the following text, I will explore what role technology can play in more subtle ways. When I look at places where the education is very much '*not broken*' it is clear to see the powerful ways that technology is being used to support and aid the organisation. When the original effectiveness research was undertaken, technology was still in its infancy. Reliable networks were just emerging in schools and colleges and the World Wide Web had only been defined by Tim Berners-Lee in the early 1990s, so the possibilities for the collaborative environments that technology has subsequently been able to support were not available. I would also note here that adding the technology dimension

Table 8.1 Technology and effective schools

	Characteristics of effectiveness	The role of technology
1	Participatory leadership	• Supports involvement in decision-making • Teachers can disseminate and share new ideas rapidly
2	Shared vision and goals	• Technology systems support 'evolutionary planning' using collaborative tools
3	Teamwork	• Supports high-quality collaboration and ensures collegiality • Teams can operate at speed
4	A learning environment	• Supports risk-taking • New ideas and pedagogies are explored
5	Emphasis on teaching and learning	• Supports adaptive practice • Widens the available repertoire • Extends learning time beyond the traditional learning day
6	High expectations	• Ensures rapid sharing of expectations • Ensures aspirations and successes are communicated
7	Positive reinforcement	• Data systems aid monitoring and provide evidence • Data systems show success and ensure recognition • Supports rapid adaption through agile IT systems
8	Monitoring and enquiry	• Data gathering and dissemination is rapidly supported • Supports ongoing review and provides evidence for discussion • Data can be used to set alerts on performance • Interventions can be speeded up by the effective use of data
9	Pupil rights and responsibilities	• Allows pupils to share views using social media • Supports pupil involvement
10	Learning for all	• Allows teachers to continue to study • Supports peer observation using video tools • Good ideas can be shared, referenced and evidenced at speed
11	Partnerships and support	• Opens the organisation to the community

to this twenty-year-old research is very much like trying to flex the industrial model. Later I'll take a more fundamental look at how systems need to reform so that technology is not some adjunct to the current system but is a fundamental enabler in building a system that is fit for the 21st century.

Leadership

Leadership is the single most important factor in every successful organisation. In my experience, outstanding Learning Organisations have strong and purposeful leaders who share expertise and insights. They enthuse the organisation with a compelling vision. They hold people to account, celebrate success and tirelessly focus on students, learning, teaching and outcomes. I have seen leaders demonstrate these characteristics in different ways in different organisations.

In terms of leadership style, I see leaders who *personalise* their leadership. They are very hands-on, they model behaviour, are very accessible and tackle everything from the big strategic issues to the everyday detail. There are leaders who *share* the leadership role by carefully choosing people to do tasks and to lead initiatives on behalf of the organisations. I see leaders who are *collegiate* in their approach. They create a team, share and refine the vision, define the tasks that need to be done and create a framework for accountability and success.

Leadership is a book on its own, and many have been written. It is useful to read and reflect on the many examples of powerful leadership, from the international figures who have shaped history to the local people who inspire local groups, no less powerfully, each and every day. Maybe the ultimate leader is one who can adapt and develop their leadership approach as an organisation grows, develops and changes over time. Certainly, one size does not fit every situation and success in one organisation does not, in my experience, guarantee success in another.

The comparison I like to make about leadership styles is between *ants* and *elephants*. Ants are incredibly busy, they can lift fifty times their own weight and cover a lot of ground very quickly. Elephants, on the other hand, take a longer view. They move that bit s . . . l . . . o . . . w . . . e . . . r and think things through. Whilst they are not as nimble as ants, they have time on their side.

Dream big, act small

Without purposeful leadership, any organisation will flounder. I was fortunate to work for IBM during the period when the company was being turned around from being in real trouble to once again becoming a global force under the leadership of Lou Gerstner. That journey is well documented and the book by Gerstner called *Who Says Elephants Can't Dance* is an interesting read.[6] Powerful leaders make things happen.

People make a difference – leaders inspire but people do the doing

Whilst leaders are essential, it's the people that make things happen. So, any organisation where the leadership eclipses the work going on day to day will probably, by definition, eventually be ineffectual. I have seen this expressed in many different ways, but two examples stick out for me.

'Dream Big, Act Small'. This was the title of a letter that Mother Teresa of Calcutta sent to her co-workers in 1987. Her message was 'Feed one hungry neighbour instead of lamenting on world hunger.'[7] In other words, the small things count. As I am sure you will know she never gave up the bigger dreams of feeding the world but she rolled up her sleeves and made a difference each and every day.

Harvard Professor of Business Rosabeth Moss Kanter talks of 'Change Masters' and 'Difficult Middles'. She talks of projects that are worthy and worth doing but that in the middle of the project it all looks very difficult and it is easy to give up. These were the difficult middles and her Change Masters were the people who did not give up and made things happen by getting involved in the big things and the little things. In her book *Evolve* she looks at many of these ideas and it is still well worth a read even though it is now several years old.[8]

Leaders use ICT differently

Senior leaders use ICT in everything they do, both as a personal pro-ductivity tool and as a tool for their organisation. ICT is not in itself a game changer, but the way it is applied by leaders to the organisation changes the game. Recently, a head teacher who was new to a school walked around taking photos of student work, displays and other things that were good about the school. He then emailed these to staff as a demonstration of the powerful learning that was going on.

Never underestimate the power of leadership. *Quality of outcomes = quality of leadership*. I would add that quality ICT supports quality leaders.

It's all quite complex

The overwhelming message that I see emerging is that the application of ICT to learning and teaching is complex. The way an organisation is led, the educational philosophy, the way teachers teach and the way the building is configured all play a very important part in defining the ICT solution that is required. Add to that the shift from institutional ICT to personal ICT and I hope we can see a landscape emerging where the factors make a bit of sense.

The further we move towards personalised learning, where we encourage learners to explore and construct their understanding whilst teachers guide, the more complex the ICT solution becomes. There is the need for tools that allow learners to create rather than simply consume – it is in the construction that they demonstrate their mastery of an idea or a topic. Learners want to construct using video and audio as well as text and static images. Video and audio place greater demands on infrastructure and create more storage demands. Video and audio have narrative value in the same way that well-written prose or verse has an impact. As we allow learners to move towards learning in longer sessions and away from strict time-bound sessions, we see the need to access their content from multiple locations. This begins to break the on-site storage model that uses the traditional client–server file storage systems. Content and the stuff they use needs to be accessible from anywhere that they have access to the Web and from any device they choose. Forget bringing your own device here, just get hold of a Web browser on any device and you are up and running and able to create as well as consume.

The Now of the Web

The 'Now of the Web' speaks to the idea of instant access; access to the tools I need and the data I need is now seamless and simple. The institutional restrictions placed on me by on-site network security are diminishing and if organisations try to restrict me I'll get around those restrictions however I can. My device is secure in that it has antivirus software and I can choose to turn on a firewall and protect myself from malicious attacks. I need to be aware of people trying to trick me into giving away my personal information but I am free to create, consume and learn. I have written the following section, 'Third Millennium

Learners', to try and direct thinking towards the young people who are the focus of the learning we talk about.

Third Millennium Learners

Hunched over a device, what are they doing? Texting, searching... learning? Our current learners are the most exquisite and expert Third Millennium Learners. They utilise technology not as a secondary adjunct but as the primary tool for exploration, consumption and presentation of ideas and topics.

They know how to consume content using the right device for consumption, they know how to create using the latest tools and the devices they need to create what they want to express. They know where to get information from and they know how to communicate in the digital universe. Mostly they are tech-savvy individuals who are carving their own learning path. In fact, the term 'tech savvy' is probably not relevant, they just know how to use the stuff and just 'get' the whole idea of the digital universe. They know about the language of video and audio in a way that the older generation know about poetry, prose and metaphor.

They instinctively know about flipped classrooms, in fact they invented the idea of learning outside the traditional classroom walls. 'Flipping' the classroom is an interesting tactic from 'Second Millennium Learners' (us oldies) to provide suitable ways to engage our Third Millennium Learners.

In this world, technology solutions in schools need to be agile, scalable and sustainable in a way they have never been before. They need to embrace the Now of the Web – where users just sign up to services and there is no long-winded debate about whether the infrastructure can support 1000–2000 users all wanting to create and access digital content at the same time.

So, our youngsters are Third Millennium Learners in terms of using and leveraging the tools they are exposed to all the time. Makes you think about what a 'Third Millennium Learning Network' needs to be able to do in the 21st-century Learning Organisation!

Just as an additional thought – these learners have a couple of other expectations. Everything these Third Millennium Learners need is 'in the cloud' – in other words, they just access it via a mobile device and it is not locked into a physical location. Also, they expect it to be free at the point of delivery. Payment is made somewhere – by advertising, selling of personal information, mobile bills – but payment is not made at the point of use in terms of handing over money each time they access their data.

And it's not just the younger generation that is embracing this world as some might have us believe. I really should have this as one the myths in the previous chapter. We constantly hear the personal IT revolution being talked about as if it is something that only the young are taking part in. Take a look around you ... if you are in a public place, look at who is using technology. If the places you frequent are anything like the places I go to then you'll see that everyone is on their device. Whether it is email, SMS or some other form of social media; Facebook, Twitter, Snapchat ... humans like to talk, share and collaborate and these tools support that in ways that we never imagined twenty years ago. The desire to communicate and talk to each other is not just for the young, it's for all of us.

Maximum impact – fit for purpose

At one extreme, access to ICT is used at fixed points in a lesson/term/year and appropriate resources can be booked and are used by everyone at the same time. There is tight control over what ICT is used for and teachers need to be able to control access to the use of resources. Students often use ICT to consume pre-prepared materials. Construction might focus more on written text using a word processor or some kind of presentation software. Images may be embedded but video and audio are not the norm. Assessment is formative.

The other extreme is where students have a very personalised path; there is a topic-based curriculum that allows learners to follow ideas and thoughts as they occur during the learning. Teachers are essential as they guide and help learners to make sense of what they are discovering. Learners may work in mixed-age groups and access teachers, mentors and other experts based on expertise and need. Spaces are flexible and specialist facilities need to be available as and when needed. There is a need to access material often in a non-linear fashion, often at very short notice. Students create and post thoughts and ideas as they work and need to pull ideas together at the end of a topic to demonstrate understanding. Assessment is summative. In-between these two extremes there are a myriad of models where ideas from the two extremes are used to meet the needs of certain topics.

At a very simple level, the teacher-led approach to learning, where things are very predictable and ICT is often used at fixed points by a traditional class, presents the best understood and in some ways most simple ICT implementation. The traditional client–server network that has been around since the late 1980s offers the facilities to support this model. Word processing and presentation software is relatively straightforward and sharing is often asynchronous and focused on handing in paper-based assignments that present the facts and knowledge that has been taught. Users have their own discrete personal areas to store documents and staff produce documents that are then placed in areas where students can access them. There is often also a high dependency on subject-focused software to support the curriculum model.

Everywhere and all the time

A learner-led, personalised model requires far more ubiquitous access to ICT. There are very few fixed points in the day where everyone uses ICT 'en masse' for the same thing at the same time. This model looks well beyond the traditional client–server network model. It draws extensively from the Now of the Web. It demands flexibility and agility to support students and teachers as they follow ideas and thoughts. Synchronous sharing of ideas between multiple learners is the focus here, as students create and share ideas and thoughts that eventually need to be pulled together into some kind of electronic scrapbook that demonstrates their mastery of a topic. Personal areas to store documents become less important as sharing and working together in groups is much more the norm – collaboration and communication become paramount so that the learning that is going on can be closely monitored and guided. Mobile, wireless and personal devices become the norm and learners pull together ideas in new and exciting ways.

How and where

How are learning spaces linked to the way learning and teaching takes place? Where does pedagogy fit in? How does this fit with the vision for the organisation? It's quite simple at one level. Create rooms for thirty people with everyone facing in one direction and you create a single focus for the room and for the learning and teaching. Create flexible spaces with up to three areas of focus and things change. Environment clearly affects learning, how teachers teach and how learners can learn. Much of this flows from the vision of the person or people leading the organisation. How much of this is overtly discussed in Learning Organisations?

Leading 21st-century companies are famous for how the vision of the leader permeates all aspects of the organisation. Google is probably the most accessible example. Their relaxed approach to office space, dress and meeting protocols, aligned with their philosophy of giving employees time to think creatively, are embedded in the organisation. Did this approach grow first and the technology come second? In this instance, the technology solution they created fed the organisational model.

In *Evolve* Moss Kanter talks of companies that transitioned from 'Bricks and Mortar' to 'Clicks and Mortar'.[9] So, changing organisations with rich histories to adopt new technologies may be harder than creating an organisation around the agile and personal mobile technologies of the late 20th and early 21st centuries.

Spare a thought for how ICT is used in schools as the spaces and the approach to learning and teaching changes . . . we'll explore that more later.

From research and observation, I have created three broad models for the way *teaching* and *learning* takes place. These models look at a *traditional* classroom-based approach, an approach where the predominant approach is *facilitation* and where learners *participate* a lot more, and a final model that is *learner-led* and *personalised*. This can then be cross-referenced against the *spaces* and *places* we looked at previously (traditional classrooms, flexible classrooms and flexible spaces).

Traditional Learning

The first model is what I have called 'Traditional Learning'. This is probably what everyone recognises as the way teaching has been taking place since the start of time, hence the use of 'Traditional Learning' as the description. In this model teachers dominate the proceedings and students are the consumers of what is being taught. The teacher has a group of same-age peers in a room. There is normally a prescribed curriculum that needs to be covered and that curriculum is broken up into a set of consumable portions that are delivered in a linear fashion, in small chunks of time over a prescribed period – a term, year, Key Stage, etc. Often what the learner has understood is tested at the end of a course using a test that is taken by each individual.

This clearly works well within the teacher-led model described earlier where learning spaces are conceived as traditional classrooms. ICT is often used to present ideas to learners and learners are encouraged to use ICT 'en masse' to present ideas or research around a topic that the teacher has introduced.

Facilitation

The next model looks at what I have called 'Facilitated Learning'. Here the learner and the teacher are taking a more equal role in the process of learning.

The emphasis for the teacher is to facilitate the learner to understand a subject or a topic. The model starts to move away from the idea of having an individual teacher and moves towards teams where each member of the team has particular strengths that are used to motivate and stimulate the learning.

The language of the teacher also moves away from simply informing or telling learners things to encouraging the learners to ask questions about how and why things are as they are.

More flexible spaces are ideally required and the delivery of the learning takes place in a less formal way. The ICT is, once again, predominantly required at the same time by the whole class, as the pace and nature of the learning is still very much happening according to a timetable prescribed by the teacher.

Participation

Here the learner is a very active participant in the learning. The learner is engaged in activities, some of which take place outside the traditional school day and off 'school' premises. A wide range of people can become involved in the learning and teaching process. Often the pre-defined path that the teacher has planned can be positively subverted by the learner as they follow an idea or thought process that would normally not be part of a topic under the other models. The environment is ideally less formal with spaces that can be used for many different activities. The emphasis on same-age peer groups begins to break down as learners access different expertise depending on their needs. Students may work with different age groups for different activities based on their understanding and proficiency in different areas of learning.

Personalised

The personalised approach places the learner at the centre of the process rather than placing the teacher at the centre. Learners are guided in this model, they are supported and helped to create links between ideas so that they build a deep understanding of an idea or a topic. Discussion and debate are a key element in this model as both learners and teachers explore and gain insights into the topics being covered.

The teacher very much guides and supports. Location and grouping of learners is much less formal with groups coming together based on their needs, understanding and enthusiasm for topics. The teacher has to use a number of higher-order thinking strategies to support and guide the learning so that the learner ultimately makes sense of the things they are discovering. ICT needs to be personal to support the individual. There are much higher demands on the ICT to provide spaces where ideas can be shared and discussed and then pulled together at a later date. How learning happens is as important as what is being learnt.

The futurologist

With my 'future' hat on I predict three things about technology: it will be mobile and, I believe, personal – it will probably be wearable, although the extent to which wearable technology pervades learning will depend on how screen technology develops; it will be wireless, leveraging the latest wireless protocols to support the fastest throughput rates; and it will be connected to the Web using some kind of browser interface and leverage the ever-expanding app ecosystem that continues to develop. Who will make the device, what operating system it will use and the exact form factor are all open for rapid change. History shows us that manufacturers change rapidly. In the late 1990s Nokia dominated the mobile market, then along came the iPhone from Apple and the world changed. With the rise of Google and Android the world is shifting again. Wearable technology is just on the edge of creating a new paradigm shift and small specialist devices that do specific things like look after your heating are rapidly emerging.

Everything is pointing towards personal devices being the norm, moving away from devices being solely owned by the organisation. This trend is quietly sweeping across all organisations, not just Learning Organisations. As with all change there is an undercurrent of resistance from various quarters. There are multiple excuses for not allowing personal devices onto existing networks. These range from fears about security to concerns with the performance of networks when the number of devices that are connected increases dramatically. This personal-device trend is, however, unstoppable. It makes no sense to me that we will, or should, stop users using their own devices.

Data, data everywhere

Not only are personal and tablet devices proliferating, but so is the quantity of data being generated, shared and 'consumed'. This is probably the most significant trend of all. Whatever the device, and however it is accessed, the use and potential for data shows how important the role of technology will continue to be in our everyday lives.

The avalanche of data we are collecting has the potential to help us understand how learners are doing in real time. Presenting this real-time picture of how learning is developing offers the potential to tailor learning in a much more individualistic way than we have ever done before. Teachers, parents and learners can look at progress and make better-informed decisions about how learning is progressing.

All surveys that look at data tell us that the quantity of data will increase exponentially over the next few years. With more and more devices tracking what is going on and sharing the data, there is an ever-growing opportunity to analyse the data to show patterns of activity that have hitherto been hidden. Monitoring performance data for learners is essential. Timely information on the success of students allows teachers and the learners themselves to understand how they are progressing. In the next twenty years the critical factors I can see is that data about how a learner is doing will be available to the learner as quickly as it is to teachers and mentors. This trend will allow learners to become much more adept at understanding how they learn and give them a much better sense of how they are performing against others in their learning cohort.

Whose data is it anyway?

Whilst we are thinking about data and personal devices we ought to think about where people will store their documents, research and other arte-facts. Since the inception of networks in Learning Organisations, users have been compelled to store their data in spaces that are owned and controlled by the organisation. That data was mostly unavailable when they were not on the physical site, and when they left the data stayed where it was, archived but unavailable to the user. But with the development of personal devices, the 'always on' paradigm of the mobile devices, the growth of the Internet and the proliferation of access to the World Wide Web, users are able to store their data in the places that they choose. This 'democratisation' of data storage is forcing organisations to face some significant issues. It comes hand in hand with the 'Bring Your Own Device' debate. Whatever the short-term issues around this are, in the longer-term users will want to use personal storage areas. Why shouldn't they? It will save costs for the organisation as less storage will be required on a network and it will allow users to take advantage of flexible and free storage plans. Their data is available when they need it and it follows them around as they move between organisations. Integrating and securing critical documents, like evidence of success, can be shared with those that need access in Learning Organisations. Even today, as I write, sharing documents with others is a fundamental facet of all cloud-based storage systems. Pulling together these factors helps to create a picture of technology that is personal, always connected, uses web-based storage and is instant. I use the term the Now of the Web to focus on the fact that users are living in a world where technology simply allows them to do things instantly, without the need to go through a gatekeeper to authorise what can or cannot be done. Once again, I am not proposing that a 'free for all' should exist. There need to be sensible levels of security, but the 'locking and blocking' culture that some organisations still insist upon will fade. Where that culture is removed first is where the learners will have the greatest advantage.

Why two devices, why two networks?

The next challenge for the future is how devices are owned, paid for and how Learning Organisations might be able to bring together what their learners are using outside the organisation. I can see no reason why in the 21st century and beyond the lines between institutional and public networks (both mobile and wireless) shouldn't continue to blur to the extent that the end user sees no difference between the two.

The critical factor in all this is the Internet and the World Wide Web. Mobile networks are of course connected to the Internet by default and from there they can access the World Wide Web. They ceased being voice-only networks many years ago, so at this level the delineation between voice and data has disappeared. However, in the majority of Learning Organisations there is still a very big gap between the on-site network and the connection to the Internet and, from there, on to the World Wide Web. Most learning networks are still being built to exist on just the physical site. They are still being built using client–server/local domain-based models that do not, by default, easily talk to Web-based systems. This is wrong and needs to be tackled. On average, a Learning Organisation will only refresh their IT network every five years. This is simply ridiculous. As I write in 2017 it was only five years ago that the tablet computer came along and changed the world. In that time, the whole world of IT has gone through several major changes. Organisations need an agile IT strategy – not one that chases the latest fashion, but one that is able to adapt and support learners' needs. We do our learners a massive disservice if we build inflexible IT systems that use twenty-year-old architectures and approaches.

Any device, any network

In the future, I believe that Learning Organisations will create relationships with mobile operators to allow a user to move seamlessly between public mobile 3G/4G (5G/6G?) connectivity, public wireless and on-site 'private' networks. To the end user there needs to be no difference when roaming between mobile cells and joining on-site networks.

The relationship between mobile providers and Learning Organisations will go further in my opinion. There is an opportunity to create commercial relationships between mobile operators and Learning Organisations. If a learner wants to upgrade or buy a new device the cost could be split between the mobile operator and the learner. The combined mobile operator/Learning Organisation could, for example, fund the device with the end user paying for offsite data use under a contract or pay as you go (PAYG) option. Lack of credit on PAYG would not preclude the user accessing the learning network whilst on site. Organisations could agree various data tariff approaches. Such an approach is a paradigm shift in the way devices and networks are perceived, funded and maintained. Thinking on this needs to start as soon as possible. Ultimately, this all points towards what I call the UMODD model – Using My Own Device and Data.

In this chapter, I have tried to share how technology sits within the ecosystem of highly effective Learning Organisations. I have also tried to share how some of the trends in technology need to be embraced rather than pushed to one side. Now is a time for emergent and breakthrough thinking that is clearly focused on making Learning Organisations really fit for the modern era. As I reflect on this chapter I would also like to reinforce how learning is now global and not just local. Much of what I refer to sits within the UK education system, but it is clear that the trends are global, and to be effective Learning Organisations need to recognise the global nature of what they are doing.

Notes

1 Schleicher, A. (2015). *Students, Computers and Learning: Making the Connection*. Paris: PISA, OECD Publishing, Page 4.
2 Schleicher, A. (2015). *Students, Computers and Learning: Making the Connection*. Paris: PISA, OECD Publishing.
3 GSMA. (2017). Definitive Data and Analysis for the Mobile Industry. Available at: www.gsmaintelligence.com [2017].
4 Schleicher, *op. cit.* (note 2).
5 White, J. & Barber, M. (eds). (1997). *Perspectives on School Effectiveness and Improvement*. London: Bedford Way Papers, Institute of Education, University of London.
6 Gerstner, L.V. (2002). *Who Says Elephants Can't Dance?* London: HarperCollins.
7 de Bertodano, T. (ed.). (1993). *Daily Readings with Mother Teresa*. HarperCollins, Page 91.
8 Moss Kanter, R. (2001). *Evolve: Succeeding in the Digital Culture of Tomorrow*. Boston, MA: Harvard Business School Press.
9 *Ibid.*

9 The system rebooted

In the Foreword, I stated that some of the underlying social truths that have been accepted for decades are being rapidly eroded. Later I explored some of those social truths and discussed how they were changing the thinking around the way learning can and will happen. Unless we act at a system level we will end up with education systems that are stranded on islands, islands that were once part of the main landmass, but that are now becoming disconnected from what learners want and need. At its worst, this disconnection creates social unrest and deeply divides society. At its best, it produces learners that are not able to immediately contribute to society and find it hard to get a job or find it hard to get a job with possibilities to progress along a career path.

History show us that change, and especially technological change, has profound effects in society. From the industrial revolution onwards, we have been inventing things that displace what has gone before. Those that embrace the change do well, those that sit in denial do less well. How we can access knowledge has changed – no debate needed. With the rise of electronic communications, we do not all need to be in the same room at the same time to learn. Arguments can be made about socialisation and the need for meeting other learners, especially around young learners, but do those who espouse that view really think that those who choose alternative learning arrangements live a totally isolated existence? This is simply not the case. Socialisation takes many forms and does not have to take place in a Learning Organisation. As we move further into the post-industrial age, work patterns will continue to evolve with portfolio careers being the norm. Being able to work in small ad hoc groups appears to be becoming the norm for the future. Therefore, flexibility and agility are key skills. In this chapter, I want to examine some of these truths and then look at how an education system that is truly fit for the 21st century might look.

What underpins the current system?

As I pull together the threads from this book and reflect on conversations and the research I have done, some fundamental issues start to be challenged time and time again, so I've summarised them here.

1) Education for all has to be funded by the state

Why? The roots of this go back to the need to ensure that everyone is able to access an education. The belief that, irrespective of your financial means, you can access education was developed and finally enshrined in law across developed societies, largely driven by the experiences of the two world wars.

In the 21st century, education must be available to all and the state has a clear role to play in that, but does this need to be entirely funded by the state or are there other models to ensure education is delivered in a cost-effective and timely way to all learners all the time? In every country, we have fee-paying schools. Parents, if financially able to do so, are willing to pay fees for their children to be educated. I always think this is slightly bizarre. Many parents openly opt for a paid route when a free option is available. I do not want to get embroiled in the political discussions around state versus private education, but there are clearly models for funding education that have yet to be explored. Article 26, paragraph 3 of the United Nations Human Rights Act of 1948 states that '*Parents have a prior right to choose the kind of education that shall be given to their children.*'[1] New models will emerge that combine state investment with private-sector investment. This has started in certain countries and will grow quickly in the latter part of the 21st century.

2) Examinations and testing

Of all the topics covered, the examination system is seen as the key inhibitor to change. No one is arguing for low-stakes testing or ditching testing, but everyone with a considered view can see that Learning Organisations are teaching to the test. This leads to a narrow view of learning that is routed in a 19th-century model and it is a global issue. I was recently fortunate enough to be invited to a session led by an educator based in the USA. His take on the issue was that the current system was set up to 'sift and sort' learners by testing what they could remember. This model was fine for an industrial society where we needed workers, managers and leaders, but for a post-industrial society where the industrial production, factory-based model has disappeared these approaches are pointless. On a wider scale, some work I was involved in that looked at the global position on curricula and testing showed that every education system is stuck in a summative testing model that then dictates what can or can't be taught and from there dictates how things should be taught. If the summative testing model could be developed then this alone would allow systems to transform very rapidly. At the end of this book I'll share ideas on how that can happen in a positive way that upholds standards and does not devalue education systems.

3) One size must fit all circumstances

Lastly, it is clear that education models must be flexible. Social circumstances change by region and, therefore, a system that dictates one approach for all is fundamentally flawed. The approach embeds failure within it as it precludes flexibility and localisation. We need to build a model where choice is built in, but choice linked to proven elements.

Reflections and the way ahead – all this got me thinking

1) Unintended consequences

For very good historical reasons, education systems in most countries are disadvantaged by history and held up by the unintended consequences of policy. Frequently in governments around the world, different parts of the government control different parts of the system, which makes change very difficult. With this comes all kinds of differences between funding arrangements, policy decisions and associated legislation.

2) What about testing?

Do education systems always support learning? There is a need to move from reporting on what learners don't know to a focus on what they do know. In Table 9.1 I present what I see as the fundamental differences

Table 9.1 Attributes of a system

Attributes	Education system	Learning system
Size	Large Learning Organisations with classrooms and specialist rooms	Small learning units as relationships are important
Knowledge organisation	Subject specialists with subject areas	Faculties based on disciplines not just single, disconnected subject areas
People structures	Hierarchical structures with clearly delineated order of seniority. Often the most senior people teach those perceived as being the most gifted	Structures exist that provide support for the faculty and discipline model, supporting discussion with learners as they encounter barriers. Groups of teachers and experts work together across boundaries
Physical environment	Learners move from area to area	Areas are equipped with the necessary resources with little need to move around. Some very specialist areas require learners to move to them, i.e. fabrication areas
Technology	Technology used for presentation and research. Controlled by the organisation and personal use is carefully sanctioned and controlled	Ubiquitous technology, with personal devices and collaboration seen as an essential component and where technology becomes a skill that is actively encouraged and taught

between a system that aims to educate and a system that aims to support learning.

Learning systems aim to create a broad canvas on to which the learner can explore their understanding and knowledge. The learning system is sensitive to the fact that in the 21st century the nature of learning is far broader than it ever was. Just knowing things is important, but is nowhere near enough. Being able to question, query and experiment are vital. These kinds of activities do not fit into traditional subject areas. The concept of disciplines emerges where multiple traditional areas of knowledge overlap to allow the learner to make sense of the complexities of the modern world.

3) Things really are different

In Table 9.2 I've looked at how the industrial and post-industrial models sit side by side. I have tried to share my emergent thinking on how our post-industrial world demands new and fresh thinking. The table needs to be read in the following way. There is an 'Elements' column on the extreme left and extreme right – these elements describe what the system might expect to see. Using the first row as an example, in the industrial world we would define a curriculum that would then be taught to learners. In the post-industrial model we would be more interested in defining the required outcomes. These outcomes are relevant and are then subject to being set against a rubric of skills and knowledge. This ensures that learning is not abstracted from real life but that it is embedded into what is required to be successful.

4) The system reimagined

Writing this book has been a revelation in many ways. From conversations and discussions with individuals to spending time researching and exploring areas and ideas that I thought I knew. However, as I wrote, researched and discussed education it became ever clearer that there was one thing that everyone was taking for granted. It was the very thing that inspired this book in the first place. It was that everyone assumed that learning belonged to schools, to education systems and that politicians had to provide the direction. I struggled for a long time to try and find a metaphor to help myself understand why this was the case. Why did society believe that learning had to be outsourced? Why was this outsourcing not delivering the outcomes that everyone wanted? One dull December day my wife and I were debating this once again over the breakfast table and suddenly a metaphor emerged that we found helpful. We likened the outsourcing of learning to the way the vast majority of the human race has outsourced food production. As we continued our discussion we reflected on the challenges this outsourcing of food production has created. The industrialisation of food production has led to a plethora of issues. From large amounts of sugar being added to processed food to large amounts of salt being added, to the waste that these systems create. The industrialisation of food production has created as many issues as it has solved. This appeared strangely close to what we are seeing with education systems. With this outsourcing of

Table 9.2 Elements of a system

	Models		
Elements	**Industrial**	**Post-industrial**	**Elements**
Curriculum	Definitive guide to the essential knowledge for the individual. Set **by** experts and subject-based	Set as part of a discussion and negotiation between key actors. These include employers, learners and teachers	Outcomes
Scheme of work	Shows how the curriculum will be covered. Usually assumes small time slots, age cohorts and an academic year	Sets out how outcomes will **be** achieved. Learners are involved in this debate and identify resources that might be required	What you need to do
Resources and content	Assumes what the learner will need and constrained **by** an approach to 'subject'-based areas and specialist rooms	What is needed to achieve the outcomes. People are also resources as are other learners of different ages	Resources
Activities	Does not feature. What learners do is of no consequence as summative testing is seen as the only evidence base upon which to judge how well the system has performed	What learners do. Actions and processes are recorded as well as outcomes. Age is not a barrier to creating new knowledge. The focus is on longer-running topic-based project work	Activities
Evidence of **out**come	Standardise tests and examinations to establish what of the curriculum has been retained	A formative record of what has been achieved. This can be used to benchmark against formal assessment vehicles if required	Verification
Delivery	In large-scale spaces, defined as spaces where greatest efficiency can **be** achieved	Where and when appropriate. Technology is essential to allow learning to take place in a flexible way and to include local, national and global resources	Delivery

food production comes this dislocation of the majority in society from being any part of food production. And so it is with learning. A large majority of parents and carers appear to have no way of participating in the learning process that their children go through. This is having the effect of making what happens in Learning Organisations ever more abstract and dislocated from what society needs. It allows educators and politicians to ignore the fundamental changes that are taking place in society.

Thinking this all through further I started to think about education in a very simple way – that of supply and demand. I am not talking about supply and demand in terms of the number of physical places that an education system needs to create to meet the number of students. That is of course important, but not my focus here. Economies thrive and businesses grow on the principles of supply and demand. At one level, things are very simple; people want things and so the market makes things and supplies them. Sometimes things are invented that no one really knew they wanted but when they see it they simply must have it and, thus, demand is created and the supply side responds. In general, demand and supply are kept in balance with the demand side having the last word in what should be provided, created and sold. Does this universal truth hold for education? Are the demand and supply side in balance? Is the supply side providing what the demand side of the equation wants and needs? Pursuing this point of view brings to the fore some intriguing and challenging points for discussion. To be clear, I see the demand side to be students and parents whilst the supply side are Learning Organisations, the majority of which are state-controlled using the taxation system to supply the funding. Looking at what the supply side delivers when you move into Learning Organisations that parents pay for directly from disposable income creates some interesting reflection points.

At a general level, one could argue that as the provision of education became less linked to the local community and more controlled by a larger state system, the further the supply side has become dislocated from the demand side. This line of reasoning opens up many interesting facets for discussion and debate – probably more than we can cover in the remainder of this chapter. But I will pull together some of the more obvious threads from other chapters to help create a centre of gravity for a debate that I hope can be developed by others as we move on through the next five years.

We know from previous data points that the demand side, our students, are involved in a world where communication and collaboration is digital and instant. From the figures that the Office for National Statistics produce on device usage to the way that digital media is being consumed, we see a very clear picture of how the demand side is engaging with the world around them. I have previously called our young 'Third Millennium Learners' and described their approach to finding things out. Others have coined different descriptors like Marc Prensky's 'Digital Natives', for example.[2] Researchers like Sugatra Mitra have sought to show us how adept our youngsters are at navigating digital systems. So, we have a clear picture of how the demand side is navigating the world, accessing information and data, and sharing and collaborating. At one level, this approach is being supported by the push for all governments to deliver services digitally as they recognise that both access to and the supply of these services can be made more efficient by adopting technology. At a summary level, the approach being adopted is digital, mobile in that location becomes less important, personal in that systems can speak to an individual rather than simply identify you as part of a group and has the attributes that allow systems to adapt quickly to change.

Now let's look at how education systems operate. Firstly, the vast majority of education systems are still analogue in nature. They operate using books and paper as the predominant form of communication between staff and students. Some use of digital devices is seen, but whilst summative examinations continue to use the paper medium, then this will persist. Most systems are still physically constrained by a building with little or no remote working or interaction. Again, exceptions start to emerge, but the tipping point will not be reached until other changes are made, as I discuss later in this chapter. The physical nature of the experience is easily explained when you think that very little weight is given to work carried out beyond the classroom. Most systems have shied away from coursework where students work on their own. The suspicion that students were receiving help from parents and others when work was being done outside the supervision of the classroom has led to the near complete removal of such tasks. Generally, the current education system is not personal. Learning Organisations are usually large because of the economies of scale. Being able to know students individually when they are one of over a thousand becomes impossible, even for those that are most adept at remembering faces and names.

The organisational structures also work from large to small. Students are part of a year group and then a class. The predominant approach is that teachers tell year groups and classes what to do and when to do it. Lastly, there is the acknowledgement that you are an individual. As we have discussed previously, these systems are also slow to change. The rhythm is that of an annual cycle that is, in turn, part of a two-, three- or five-year cycle which follows the cycles dictated by the examination system.

Therefore, change in education systems is slow and often poor practice gets embedded into a system and there are few if any drivers for change. At the level of individual schools, the external factors that push for change often come from an inspection regime that seeks to judge the organisation against summative outputs. Therefore, when change happens the focus is on these summative outputs. This forces the focus on change to be about doing those things better that improve examination or test results. Reflection on the broader change agenda can be ignored and the push is back to classrooms, teachers and remembering things that can be reproduced in an exam setting. As I have written elsewhere, it is wrong to turn and blame leaders for this response to change. Whilst we continue to judge in terms of these outcomes then leaders are forced to focus on the things that make a difference in those areas. I referenced the research on school effectiveness elsewhere and those factors, when brought to bear in a systematic way, create a high-quality system that focuses on preparing learners for these high-stakes examinations. I think of this as an example of something that is not wrong, but neither is it completely right. As an aside to this and to illustrate the point that I am addressing, I recently saw an advertisement for a job at a global corporation. The corporation in question is recognised as an employer that many would aspire to work for and offers a broad range of opportunities, good conditions of employment and great prospects for the future. The advert described the nature of the role and then said that although there was an office space the focus was on outputs and the successful person could work anywhere that they felt comfortable, mentioning a home office, the local coffee shop or the company office. The reflection I make is that this is the world our learners will inhabit. I appreciate that students of younger ages cannot just be left to wander the streets to find somewhere to work – that is not the point of this discussion. The point is that we do need to get our learners ready for a world where they will be expected to have the self-discipline to work in a variety of locations and in a variety of ways. More and more businesses are looking at their costs and realising that dedicated office spaces are expensive. Heating, lighting, desks, cleaning and security all cost money. With systems and data held securely in cloud solutions, using alternative working locations that provide Wi-Fi and electricity, are heated and where refreshments are easily available makes perfect sense. Having the necessary skills to collaborate remotely and the self-discipline and strategies to be able to concentrate in these locations are skills that people need to acquire. Reflection is needed to ensure that we understand what these changes mean and that we build in the necessary skills and competencies that people need to be successful.

Reflecting and focusing on what needs to change in education systems and making those links is challenging. It is often easy to dismiss the previous argument for a number of well-argued reasons so that the justification for the current system remains intact. I would stress that I am not talking about dismantling education systems. I wish to focus on how to make change happen that keeps high-quality learning as the core of what people do, but does that in a way that is both relevant to learners and ensures that they can move into the workplace and become highly effective. As we look at how to 'reboot' an education system that is fit for our current age *and* can be responsive to the ongoing rapid change, I suggest that we must look at three critical areas. An examination of these areas will allow us to build a deeper understanding of how the supply and demand side can be brought together into a system that both serves the needs of society whilst leading learners forward to build new knowledge and understanding.

To make sense of the changes there are two perspectives that need to be examined. In Chapter 10 I highlight some key elements that are stopping progress. These elements are mostly political and need debating because they are the barriers that are stopping rapid change taking place in the three areas I highlight in the following paragraphs. It is worth cross-referencing these three areas with the elements explored in the following chapter. By addressing the areas for change in this way, I have attempted to create an agenda for reform that asks significant questions for our leading education thinkers whilst also challenging our politicians to start having practical and pragmatic discussions about the areas where they can make a difference. If these two broad areas of debate can be triggered simultaneously, I believe they will complement each other and we could create the circumstances under which rapid and meaningful change can take place. The time frame for this change will then fit better with the speed of change in society. As noted elsewhere, I would stress again that change is not a destination; change is an ongoing process. Once triggered, it is essential that the factors that affect change are constantly reviewed and that, rather than constantly asking ourselves 'Do we need to change?', we ask 'What change do we need to activate today?' The mindset for the latter requires enquiry, looking outwards and asking questions of everyone involved in the process of education.

For our educationalists, there are three critical areas that need to be reflected on urgently. These are:

1   How do we intend to support our young people to learn? This is primarily a discussion about pedagogy. A rebooted system must recognise and understand that how we can access knowledge continues to rapidly change and, as such, the methods by which an educator and an education system works with learners will substantially change. The way our learners are accessing knowledge is changing and this must be embraced and not ignored. If we ignore the possibilities and potential that these changes to access methods present then we potentially slow our ability as a species to innovate and build solutions to some of the great challenges that lie ahead. This element of the system is attracting focus but not in perhaps the most obvious way. Many edtech start-ups are focusing on how what is being called artificial intelligence (AI) can be leveraged to better understand how people learn. AI can be best understood by looking at machine learning and understanding the areas of machine learning that combine to build an AI solution. This topic deserves more time and space than we can give it here, but, essentially, the argument is that we can use computational algorithms to better analyse what learners are doing and from that analysis can define a more personalised approach to learning that builds on strengths and addresses weaknesses. Much of what AI in edtech is doing is combining the pedagogy element with the next element – what we teach.

2   What are we going to teach to young people? As I have commented elsewhere, a detailed and thorough examination is required of the current approach to how we construct a curriculum. Critical elements like literacy and numeracy and deep knowledge must

remain, but the context within which these things are taught, referenced and practiced must be examined. There needs to be a deep
understanding of how the access to content is changing and that in
turn must lead to a thorough rethinking of what has to be told to
learners and what learners can now be expected to find out for
themselves. This element is bound tightly to how we examine our
learners. The current summative approach is stifling both what we
teach and how we teach. One could argue that the examination of
learning is the starting point for reform, but I believe that to start
there simply builds on current prejudices and does not allow for a
clarity of thinking around that problem. If we examine how we can
approach learning and then what we need to know, then the way we
access progress naturally flows from there. One can argue that an
examination system is subservient to the curriculum. Certainly, the
way we approach the creation of examinations at the moment is to
produce a syllabus that comprises a subset of knowledge that an
education systems dictates should be taught. Thus, the way we
examine mimics the way we currently approach our teaching.
Therefore, to liberate an examination system, it is necessary to liberate the way we teach and take a detailed look at what we teach.

3   Where do we see education taking place and how does this sit with
the local community? As people gain greater flexibility in how and
where they work, the nature of local communities changes. People
have more time to input to the community and the nature of the
input changes with access to high-quality skill sets with highly
motivated parents and community members being willing and
able to add significant value. Often the focus for looking at where
we teach is taken as the buildings we use as schools, colleges and
universities. The design and layout of these buildings has become a
focus for many systems. Organisations looking to transform education often look to a redesigned building to become a catalyst for
change. Whilst this appears a logical place to start, it can create
significant problems that lead to poorer outcomes. If how we
teach does not change and what we teach does not change then
creating a building that has open spaces rather than discrete classrooms, that has areas where approaches to learning are perceived to
be focused around projects and topics rather than discrete subjects
and where teachers are encouraged to work in teams rather than as
individuals, then we create tensions that result in the breakdown of

effective learning. Many reforms fail because of these tensions, and where isolated examples appear to thrive, the change process is seen as not scalable across a system.

To be clear, this rebooting is challenging. We do not regularly talk to teachers about their personal pedagogical preferences. For many, teaching is an innate and deeply personal experience. The very best teachers, like the very best athletes, are just good at what they do – better than most others at what they do, as they fully engage their learners. Sport holds some interesting reflection points. Over the last few decades athletes have begun to analyse how they perform and from that analysis coaches have created training regimes that focus on technique. The outcome of that work is athletes who are aware of why they are faster or stronger. They hone their technique until they become better at what they do. Our education systems need to spend more time working with teachers to understand pedagogy. Pedagogy is often overlooked because our current approach to curriculum, and, therefore, to examinations, is one that assumes teaching is predominantly didactic; that is, a pedagogy that is about telling people things and then checking that they can remember. Once they demonstrate their ability to remember, there is some checking that the knowledge can be applied. Therefore, the predominant pedagogy is focused on a relationship between a teacher and thirty pupils in a classroom – that method, we think, is the best way to transfer knowledge when efficiency is also considered. Our inspection systems assume this approach will be the norm and declare success or failure around that model. Our curriculum assumes this model and our buildings assume this model.

From a broader discussion around pedagogy flows the essence of a changed system. Working in teams with the wider community requires a different approach to pedagogy, as does working across subject boundaries, and assessing how these approaches have allowed learners to absorb and synthesise knowledge requires an understanding of the most effective pedagogies. I have already quoted considerably from the Foreword of the 2015 OECD book, *Students, Computers and Learning*. In essence, the book can be summarised as follows: if you give learners technology as part of the learning process, it makes no difference to what they remember when you put them in front of a piece of paper with a pencil to take an exam. The gross oversimplification of a very interesting book is an attempt to focus on the issues we face. Putting a human runner next to a powerful car and seeing which can travel along a straight one-kilometre road the fastest is a futile experiment, assuming both person and vehicle are maintained and fuelled for the journey. Despite the rise of mechanical transport, we still highly value those who can run fast or can run long distances at speed. A reformed system is not about throwing away what we value; it is about understanding that in the modern world there are new opportunities to do certain things better. Having access to mechanical transport devices (cars/trains/planes) allows us to work at distances from our homes that previously would have been impossible. That allows us to bring together people who would otherwise never meet. This makes a difference and allows us to make progress.

In rebooting our system, we therefore need to efficiently and effectively understand pedagogy and how that opens up ideas for approaching learning. I have referenced various pedagogies and what they support in Table 2.2 (see Chapter 2). We then need to review our curricula and understand what needs to be taught and what we expect our learners to find out for themselves – I have explored that further in Chapter 2. And lastly, we need to build and refurbish our buildings so that we exploit our pedagogical insights and the willingness of the community to be more involved in the education process. From this will flow an obvious and effective way of examining progress and benchmarking what people know, how they can apply what they know and how that application is leveraged to bring about new insights into problems. None of these things are new or particularly complex. They are, however, currently mostly exempt from examination because they have been carried out for so long in the same ways. Discussion about pedagogy spills over into an argument about standards and what needs to be taught rather than being seen with clarity. The design of a building, especially a design that creates open spaces, is not explicitly linked to discussions around pedagogy and curriculum design. Therefore, many reforms fail, not because they are bad or poor, but because the necessary cross-organisational discussions do not take place.

Notes

1 United Nations. (1948). Universal Declaration of Human Rights. Available at: www.un.org/en/universal-declaration-human-rights/ [2017].
2 Prensky, M. (2001). *Digital Natives, Digital Immigrants*. Available at: http://marcprensky.com [2017].

10 And so to the future

My hope at the end of all this is that three things will happen. Firstly, the places where the system has changed will be regarded with interest and wisdom, and informed discussion will take place about how places where positive change is happening can be developed into trends that sweep across mainstream education. Secondly, that the discussion will focus on how systems transform to focus on learning and the skills that are essential for the 21st century. Thirdly, that political doctrine is removed from the debate; we can stop the posturing between the teaching profession and government and focus on the learners. When I started teaching in 1984 I recall colleagues going on strike in my first year of teaching and now, thirty years later, the same issues seem to be appearing. Surely systems can move beyond the need to set up barriers around which conflict is shaped? I don't doubt the passion that we all hold for our education systems, but when that passion boils over into conflict we have lost an essential element of what learning is about – debate, discussion and informed decision-making.

The tipping points for change are clear to me and I believe the ability to move education systems forward sits in the hands of three constituencies. These constituencies are: 1) government ministers who control the levers that can change the way we constitute education systems, test and assess learners; 2) leading educationalists who advise ministers, be it formally or informally; and 3) the communities and learners themselves, who must express what they need to achieve the ambitions for the individual and the local community. If a community wishes to retain their young to be an active part of their future then the community must actively engage in shaping the learning that is available so that it offers the young the opportunities to remain in the area. Each group needs to reflect the way society is developing and to turn what they see into meaningful discussion and dialogue, and then from dialogue into actionable policy and practice. And this dialogue, policy and practice needs to happen rapidly, with the understanding that as soon as we have one set of updated policies in place then a dialogue needs to start about the next iteration. Our societies are moving quickly and this needs to be reflected in education policy. At the level of central government, it is also pertinent to reflect that the way policy is formed and implemented needs to change. Currently, policy creation and implementation can be a slow and exhausting process. Whilst due diligence and attention to detail are important, they should not be used to slow down implementation.

As I write I still perceive a view that our education systems have to stay as they are and that any significant reform will undermine standards. But when the evidence from international comparisons of education, such as the Programme for International Student Assessment (PISA), show that doing more of the same appears to be making little, if any, difference within developed systems, then the time has come to make a significant shift. History is littered with examples of greatness emerging when courage was summoned to take a step to radically reform a system. Despite all the challenges facing the UK NHS, it still provides the best care for free at the point of delivery anywhere in the world and is the envy of many nations. The steps that were needed to originally create the NHS are the kinds of change we now need to see in our education systems. The vision that created the United Nations and the Declaration of Human Rights was momentous and has shaped our world for the better. And the vision and consensus that was created around such great reform needs to emerge for our education systems at both national and global levels. If we are to build and develop systems that revolve around learning then the challenges of what Learning Organisations need to look like must be discussed and the new ideas that are being formulated need to be rapidly implemented.

Why is change so hard? So much promising education reform gets caught up in factional infighting, to such an extent that good ideas get side-lined whilst individuals and organisations appear to argue over things that are not core to the debate. Social media is alive with controversial comments that undermine much of the good that is going on. Think tanks produce ideas and research but they are frequently funded by those with a political agenda and, therefore, the research can be used to prove or disprove a political point. There are very few independent education organisations that can think and reflect on what is important. The Sutton Trust, based in the UK, has funded some very interesting and insightful research that gets to the heart of some key issues, from the work on the impact of pupil premium investment to the ongoing review of how chains of schools are having an impact on outcomes. The research they commission is rooted in looking at the social challenges society presents and tends to provide a clear and concise review of the key issues backed up with well-researched data. Also, the UK Education Foundation produces reports that are founded on high-quality research and focus on how real change can take place. There are others that also focus on the key issues.

It is worth reflecting back on leadership at this point. We know that leadership is an essential tenant for excellence wherever an organisation is seen to be thriving. Education is no different. We need education leaders who are inspired by learning and not just by meeting or aligning with the latest political direction. The challenges are not to be underestimated. If you are judged as being successful by a system that focuses on summative examinations then the necessity to meet those criteria whilst also creating a high-quality learning experience are not to be underestimated. The two are not mutually exclusive, but it can be extremely challenging at times to reconcile the two aims, especially in periods of rapid change. The challenge for our education leaders is that we need an education system that is reconceived for the modern era – one that embraces all that the modern world has to offer and one that has, at its core, the need to constantly reflect on what changes. Above all, we need a system that knows how to remain relevant. We need leaders who can see beyond the moment, leaders who can interpret the trends that are shaping society and ensure that they reconceive the system to adjust for those changes. We need to rapidly move away from prescriptive models that work in one place, are replicated elsewhere, but do not then take account the social context of the place where the model is being replicated. We need a system that is agile, listens, reflects and is capable of creating new models as they become necessary.

The stalemate in education is not unique; I see parallels in other areas too. The music industry resisted the new paradigm of streamed and downloadable music. It took a mass defection by end users to change the thinking. Once the people who used to purchase physical tapes, records and CDs started illegally sharing music and the record companies saw their revenues dropping, a change occurred. Over a very short period of time, digital copies of music and video became available and the era of streaming was born. We now expect to get music, video and TV from streamed and online sources. Some artists saw this coming – David Bowie and Prince both embraced the change rather than fighting against it. There are still areas where the industry resists change. The way success is measured for recording artists continues to change. There is still a push to recognise physical sales of music above streaming. The weekly charts that report the popularity of music are varied in the way they view streaming and physical sales. At the time of writing, the UK chart system counts 1000 streams as being equivalent to a physical sale, although the system is somewhat more complex than that. The discussion ranges between whether the charts should reflect how popular a track or artist is in terms of how often something is listened to, or whether the charts should reflect the sales of new artists, focusing on the popularity of those musicians emerging into the popular consciousness. The domination of the charts by one artist is seen as stopping new acts breaking through because funding the creation of new material does not take place. The debate continues and change is now relatively quick to take effect in the way measurement is taken. Currently, views of music videos on YouTube do not feature in these rankings, but some of the figures are remarkable. Leading artists are seeing billions of views of their music. Ed Sheeran, popular at the time of writing, has had nearly 2 billion streams of his hit song 'Shape of You'.[1] The track 'Despacito' by Luis Fonzi which has taken the world by storm has been streamed 4.6 billion times.[2] This is an incredible number when sales of Ed Sheeran's physical CD at the same point in time are 1.22 million. The nature of the disruption that digital channels are having is still not fully appreciated in my opinion. Similarly, we are seeing the watching of linear television broadcast declining with the rise of streaming and on-demand services becoming dominant. Business models are changing for broadcasters, with new organisations emerging that were previously not involved in broadcasting. Amazon and Netflix are redefining the way we interact with content as part of a broader package of interaction that revolves around the choices we make when we purchase goods and services. The way programmes are being made and conceived is changing as viewing habits change. The traditional weekly linear episode of popular formats still persists, but the way these are being consumed is very different. A detailed analysis of these changes is best left for others to comment upon, but the clear outcome of the research data is that habits are changing very fast. Empowered by technological developments, people are able to choose how and when they consume. As people choose we see that the traditional patterns for consumption, dictated by the necessity of analogue delivery systems, are not the preferred approach.

What is the equivalent in education? The trends are not as clear, but there are two indicators that point to some of the broader changes. As I write this book we are seeing a growing trend for parents opting to take children out of school in England as a protest against 'over testing'. There is also a growing trend for parents to look at educating their children at home – a common occurrence in the past, but one that appears to create controversy in our current society. The pattern for choosing alternative ways to educate is developing quickly. It is worth noting that some countries make home education illegal, taking the view that only the state can provide the necessary educational facilities for young people. This debate also quickly becomes mired in political rhetoric. Many view opting out of the education system as a very dangerous choice and argue that the state should compel all children to attend school, or at least that the state should regularly inspect in some way the education provision that children receive. We see a variety of opinions being expressed. An article in *The Telegraph* in 2016[3] takes perhaps a more measured view to alternative education options – a view that does not immediately condone such options as subversive, as they have been seen in the past, but as a serious option. Will it take a significant mass of parents opting out of the 'outsourcing' of education to make politicians and educators reach the tipping point? As job patterns change and general work patterns allow greater flexibility, then the possibility to move back to a local pre-industrial model for education becomes feasible. With broadband connectivity and the growth of online learning materials, the potential for 'insourcing' your family learning increases. The ability to connect online with experts becomes ever more feasible and the opportunity to develop a blended approach to learning in the family home or at the heart of a local community becomes a realistic proposition.

Daring to think differently

I did not want this to be just another book about education. I did not want it to become pigeonholed as a text that tried to make the case for technology in learning. That case is already made by the actions of people every day. The writing of this text and the associated research was punctuated by periods of deep review about what was going on in Learning Organisations every day. The question emerges around what an education system might look like if we were to really rethink the ways in which we construct an education system that has learning at its heart. If we believe that learning belongs to everyone then we should put learning back in the hands of everyone and from there create a system that builds outwards towards what society and the state can offer. A belief in the importance of families and communities must remain central and undiminished, and learning should be fun and exciting, grounded in what people are going to need to do to be successful in their future lives. The changes we've explored in the text to date begin to point to a new model, one that is focused on learning. One where learning can once again belong to everyone and where the role of parents and the community can be positively focused to create an exciting and rigorous model for what people learn. The challenge of overcoming the ingrained expectations that education is the remit of the state are significant. The research tells us that the use of mobile devices is ubiquitous for the demographic of young learners and their families. As previously cited, the statistics also tell us that the ownership and use of personal digital devices is almost ubiquitous for those up to forty-five years of age. We also know from research that the way these devices are being used lends itself to the delivery of great learning and we know that families and groups love doing things together.

Creating the vision for a new system is not something that can be taken lightly. As I researched for this book I took time to talk to a wide range of people, from leading thinkers to ex-ministers of state, and the discussions were fascinating. Some were working to change the current system from within, creating new ways of channelling funding and creating iterations of the current system. Such an organisation is the Oasis chain of academies. Their vision is set by Steve Chalke, a Baptist minister. Chalke has a strong and clear vision for schools being rooted deeply in the local community and working across social support systems to provide a holistic and supportive learning system. Others were looking for radical change and some were able to comment very effectively on the areas in which the current system was failing but were less clear on how changes could take place and what a new system might look like.

Elements for change

Building on the discussion in the previous chapter, I have listed in the following subsections some critical elements that I believe need to addressed to achieve far-reaching change in acceptable time frames. This is a challenge of considerable proportions, and so not to be taken lightly. These areas, when combined with the discussion in the Chapter 9 on *pedagogy, curriculum* and *where learning takes place*, build a framework for debate. In the following subsection, I have outlined the key elements that currently appear to have a stranglehold on education reform. These are areas that I believe need to be addressed at the political level rather than our educators addressing the elements, as outlined previously. The elements outlined below are ones where quite subtle changes in the way we think and act could bring about exceptional reform in relatively short periods of time.

1) Clearly define where politics and education meet

Whilst education is completely controlled by politicians, there will always be a short-term view of reform that is tied to a political cycle which is normally no more than five years. Take into account the time it takes to get policy passed then most political cycles are less than four years. Therefore, the first element for change is to find ways to remove the short-term political cycle from education reform. Whilst politicians must have a role in education systems, this role should be tempered and underpinned by trusted and proven expertise in education and learning. Whilst everyone has an understanding of education at one level because they all experienced an education themselves, this does not on its own make them an expert. As in all things, studying and understanding an area is essential for expertise to emerge. State education systems should create a transparent and representative national body that is responsible for setting the direction for the education system. The body should contain learners of varying ages, national figures who have led successful reform, parents, industry leaders and the politicians of the day. This body should not be an impotent talking shop, but should run focused sessions that map out an evolving five-year strategy that is reviewed and refined each year. Politicians would and should be able to voice their ideological views, but these views should be tempered with the perspective and understanding of others. Funding for reforms and change should be transparently debated with an honest and open brokerage taking place between vision, expectation and funding. I am not proposing a utopian committee that sits and talks. The vision is for a robust and agile group that takes evidence from what is happening on the ground and translates that into approaches that can be replicated locally, informed by local need and requirements.

2) Change the examination system

The aim is to create a push and pull on how we reflect what learning has taken place. In Chapter 9 I urged our educators to rethink how we judge learning by looking at how and what we teach. Here I am urging our politicians to debate what an acceptable examination system should look like. The element is high on everyone's agenda. Wherever discussions about education change take place the recurring theme I hear is that examination systems are the biggest break on reform. I have covered this thinking previously so I will not go over this ground again. However, to summarise: testing is required to set benchmarks and ensure standards. But the need for every area of learning to tested by a summative paper-based exam is dead. Simply moving those examinations online misses the point. A reformed examination system must look at the skills we require to be successful and seek to benchmark the learner in demonstrating those skills. Again, I have discussed the range of skills previously, but, briefly, literacy and numeracy are essential but not in isolation. Testing numeracy and literacy as part of a task is essential. The application of knowledge to a problem is essential so testing a learners' ability to apply knowledge is essential. Testing must also recognise that in the modern world the sequence by which a learner gains understanding can be less linear that in the past. With the ability to rapidly find things out, the learner can be challenged to tackle problems that require knowledge and expertise they have not yet mastered. Building in opportunities to allow them to acquire new knowledge and skills is essential in any examination system. Finally, taking a longitudinal view of a learner's acquisition of skills is important. Successful people never stop learning and we should be building a system that challenges and tests how a learner manages their learning over a period of time. This should include self-review and evidence of strategies to acquire and develop new skills. Flexibility is key, along with clear strategies to research and find things out, explore new areas and to always be questioning the status quo. As discussed in Chapter 9, change in an examination system will flow from a review of pedagogy and curriculum content, so, whilst reviewing an examination system in isolation is essential, it is still part of the broader picture I discussed previously. Change could be driven by altering the examination system, but change is much more likely to take place at speed if the discussions on pedagogy, curriculum and where learning happens are also going on simultaneously.

3) Build from the community outwards

The time of the state mandating and expecting people to blindly follow has gone. The democratisation of knowledge via digital channels has created a world where access to knowledge is easy. Therefore, argument and debate happens more freely and opinions are formed more quickly. Local communities can be informed and empowered in ways that are only just becoming clear. The lifespan for politicians that sit in the centre of a nation and push out policy is severely limited. Education policy must engage from the local community and build outwards. The role of politicians elected to represent communities at a national assembly is to reflect and deftly ensure that local needs are met. The learning that is needed by the local community must be available and supported by national strategies. But these strategies have to take account local needs. Time frames need to be shortened for policy implementation and funding must be able to effectively reflect local needs. As we all become more flexible in how, when and where we work, these changes are essential. We hear many predictions that thousands more jobs will be replaced by automation. Therefore, we will have an ever-growing pool of well-educated and motived local people who can, and should, be actively involved in the learning experiences of the young. Building outwards from the community and engaging nationally where appropriate is an essential prerequisite for any modern education system that operates in a state of moderate size or bigger. It is useful to reflect that many people are looking at smaller states like Singapore and Norway as models for how reform can happen. Their education systems appear to be flexing to take account of change but their size is also relevant. One could argue that they are closer in size to local communities in larger states and that change is, therefore, much more reflective of local needs. There are lessons here, but maybe not the ones we have so far looked to embrace. The current wisdom is that we should look at what these smaller states are doing to try and replicate those changes across a lager system – but does this miss the point of size and flexibility?

4) The state provides resource, expertise and support

Governments collect taxes, so the provision of education from a tax system will remain a function of government, and it needs to be to ensure that universal education is available. The state also needs to show that expenditure is creating acceptable outcomes. However, the state should, and could, delegate more effectively on how education funding is distributed. Much of the state's role in current education systems is focused on looking at standards as they are currently conceived. This should be reviewed and the state should play a greater role in facilitating the kinds of discussions that are required to frame reform. Currently, the only places where teachers talk about reform are at conferences that are often sponsored by companies with an agenda. National and regional debate for and by teachers that feeds into policy is often limited. Such discussions need not be cumbersome or complex. Ideas can be shared quickly and simply using numerous technology systems. Collating and creating consensus around key themes can be done quickly and effectively. Many commercial organisations have created internal ways to elicit and share ideas to inform strategy – this approach is simple and effective, and would give central government a clear insight into how educators perceive the world around them. Teachers are sharing ideas using technology as the conduit and the state needs to tap into these debates, lead these debates, collate feedback and move reform forward from this interaction.

5) Technology is a given and education is 'digital by default'

Every country and region should have a defensible and pragmatic digital education strategy. The strategy should not talk in terms of the technology itself, but should focus on and recognise the changes that technology is causing and look at how to embed those changes into the way Learning Organisations operate. Having a digital strategy is not about the devices being used or the underlying networks that are needed, it is about understanding how a digital world changes the way we collaborate and share – how technology creates new opportunities and changes existing paradigms. Creating the right level of dialogue that focuses on the real changes is essential and avoiding device-level discussions is paramount. Discussions about the relevance of personal digital devices are essential and building positive models for use are paramount. This area of debate is currently lacking; focus continues on the device itself, not on how collaboration changes.

6) Rethink physical buildings

It is not necessary to abandon traditional buildings, but it is essential to think about how the use and function of spaces need to change. Many of these changes will flow from how the community engages in the process. Also, we are pretty much still working with the traditional paradigm of one teacher to thirty pupils in most systems. There is potential for this to change, as discussed in Chapter 9. Moving to an approach where exploration and collaboration are examined will necessitate a change to the way teaching takes place. As I have commented in earlier chapters, the way learning happens can change from a predominantly teacher-led approach, because we are looking at simply passing a summative examination, to a system where we need to measure and understand the collaboration process. This will be seen as a profound change for many and should not be interpreted as an abandonment of standards in the areas of numeracy and literacy. It is too simple to reject change in this way. As Andreas Schleicher points out,[4] simply adding 21st-century approaches to traditional pedagogies will not yield the outcomes we seek.

There is a need for flexibility and agility in the way we approach change and reform. As previously discussed, one size does not fit all, and local variation will be needed. To be clear, I am not simply rehearsing the rationale for community schools as they have been previously conceived. I am asking for a deeper look at how a Learning Organisation sits in the centre of the community and how it becomes a realistic and accessible resource for the entire local community.

Therefore, our rebooted system seeks to embed flexibility at its core, where digital strategies are at the heart of systems so that communication and collaboration can be fully embedded into the way we interact with learners. We understand and talk about pedagogy, we understand why we teach what we teach and we understand why we design buildings the way we do. Local communities are critical and, using a variety of strategies, parents and others can become involved in what happens in Learning Organisations much more easily than at present. Systems that judge learner progress are rigorous, but factor in skills of collaboration and communication as key elements of the overall judgement of success. Learners and educators have access to high-quality data that allow critical decisions to be made about progress. Where challenges are detected, they can be addressed, and where progress is clear, this can be celebrated. Building a system that is responsive to ongoing change is essential; nothing stands still and in five years' time we will have the tools and strategies to enable the highly sophisticated analysis of performance and progress. As the sum total of human knowledge increases, the nature of the problems we seek to solve will become ever more complex. A single individual will not be able to solve these issues, so working with others using highly developed collaboration skills will be the norm.

Finally, in closing, it is against this backdrop of learning that I would like this book to be judged. The time is right for the redefinition of a system, but that redefinition needs to be made against the needs of communities and individuals, not against the needs of a state system that looks to the past. The modern world is creating such opportunity for our young people that we must act, and act quickly. The research and analysis for this book has taught me many new things. The single most inspiring thing is the way that our young people are embracing change in a positive way. They are taking advantage of developing education systems to access learning as never before. They are using technology to make themselves smarter, do things faster and be more efficient. At a global level, we are moving ever closer to being able to provide an education for every child. Where we have universal education provision we are making great strides in creating smarter people who will go on to solve some of the big challenges we will face in the future. The challenge for more established education systems, where universal access to education is firmly established, is how to make the next big change. The time is right for a significant step forward. Reform should be embraced so that in five years' time we have systems that are fit for purpose and equip our learners with the skills they need to be successful.

Notes

1 Sheeran, E. (2017). Shape of You. YouTube. Available at: www.youtube.com/watch?v=JGwWNGJdvx8 [2017].

2 Levine, N. (2017). 'Despacito' Is Now the Most Streamed Song Ever. Available at: www.nme.com/news/music/despacito-now-streamed-song-ever-2113022 [2017].

3 Gordon, O. (2016). Hating the New SATs? Meet the Mums Who Chose Home Education Over 'Sausage Factory' Schools. Available at: www.telegraph.co.uk/women/family/hating-the-new-sats-meet-the-mums-who-chose-home-education-over/ [2017].

4 Schleicher, A. (2015). *Students, Computers and Learning: Making the Connection*. Paris: PISA, OECD Publishing.

About the author

I've been working in education for over thirty years. I spent half of that time teaching in a range of schools in the maintained education sector. Having that grounding in classrooms as a teacher of maths, music and IT created a love for learning. I worked in some amazing schools and used early computers in my learning, including Commodore Pet, BBC micros, Acorn Risc PCs, Apple, IBM PCs and Atari ST machines as the basis for an early midi-based recording studio. I would have happily continued teaching if it were not for a set of circumstances that saw me moving to work for IBM for six years. I went to IBM to support an EMEA research programme called Reinventing Education. This programme exposed me to education systems across the world and I met and worked with some very talented individuals who were literally reshaping our world. My time at IBM also gave me an insight into the world of change management. In the early 2000s I left IBM and ran the IT department for a large group of independent schools in the UK, and I subsequently worked for one of the most successful groups of academies as it grew very quickly. In both those roles I was able to combine my knowledge of education with my understanding of technology to build scalable and flexible systems that have stood the test of time. In 2013, I moved on to be the director of a UK-based SME that provided IT services to education. We built a private cloud environment for education that provided IaaS, PaaS and SaaS services. It grew rapidly and provided a range of services to a diverse range of organisations.

In 2015, I started my own company and embarked on a series of projects and ideas working with people who want to change the world through learning. The Original Group continues to grow and work with a wide range of individuals and organisations that are focused on doing things that have not been done before. Our goal is quite simple – we want to change the world and bring back the love of learning to everyone.

Index

Locators in *italics* refer to figures and those in **bold** to tables.